THE SENCO HANDBOOK

Working within a Whole-School Approach

FOURTH EDITION

Elizabeth Cowne

David Fulton Publishers
London

David Fulton Publishers Ltd
The Chiswick Centre, 414 Chiswick High Road, London W4 5TF

www.fultonpublishers.co.uk

David Fulton Publishers is a division of Granada Learning Limited, part of Granada plc.

First edition published in 1996 by David Fulton Publishers
Second edition 1998
Third edition 2000
Fourth edition 2003
10 9 8 7 6 5 4 3 2

The right of Elizabeth A. Cowne to be identified as the author of this work has been asserted by her in accordance with the Copyright, Designs and Patents Act 1988.

Copyright © Elizabeth Cowne 2003

British Library Cataloguing in Publication Data
A catalogue record for this book is available from the British Library.

ISBN 1 84312 031 3

Typeset by Textype Typesetters, Cambridge
Printed and bound in Great Britain by The Thanet Press, Margate

Contents

Foreword

School SEN Coordinators (SENCOs) were once optional extras. Now virtually every school has a SENCO and the Code of Practice (2001) even insists they are to be paid out of the core budget of the school.

The legal and regulatory spotlight on the SENCO's role has shown that the women and men holding these important posts are often working alone, or nearly alone. They need training, support and time to do the job.

The author of a book supporting the SENCO's work must be someone with great practical expertise and understanding of schools, a commitment to achieving the best for all pupils and the ability to take a broad view, in relation to both historical developments and national, local and individual school systems.

Liz Cowne meets all the criteria. She has a long background in mainstream school work with SEN, and has been involved since 1983 in innovative teacher training for SENCOs at the Institute of Education, University of London. Liz Cowne has been able to review practice since 1993 nationally and across the many schools she knows well. She has drawn out the key issues and difficulties. She can offer full discussion of the issues and provide solutions that she has seen working in schools.

I particularly welcome the attention Liz Cowne gives to curriculum, both in its broadest sense and in the narrower definition delineated by the National Curriculum. If pupils with special educational needs are to achieve their entitlement from recent legislation for education, a proper understanding of the place of every teacher and of the classroom in the task is essential. Liz is particularly well placed to tackle these issues as she has been a consultant on SEN and curriculum for the Qualifications and Curriculum Authority (QCA).

Liz Cowne's ability to provide a theoretical context to practical ideas is shown at its best in her discussion of the role of the Individual Education Plan in relation to whole curriculum design. She suggests that we need to be careful that a device for action on priorities for individuals does not draw us to a narrow viewpoint.

The SENCO, of course, is not just a hands-on operator. Through her skill in professional development and support other teachers grow and develop their practice in relation to special educational needs. Liz Cowne explores all this and, to offer support to supporters, presents some well tested staff development models for readers to try.

I am delighted to introduce this book and its author to the reader. It will take her only a few pages to show you what a good friend she is to those who take on the challenging task of SENCO – and to all those children and young people whose learning SENCOs seek to enhance.

Nick Peacey, Coordinator, SENJIT,
Institute of Education, University of London,
December 2002

Acknowledgements

The author would like to thank the many colleagues who have contributed inspiration to, or advice on, the writing of this book. I owe the original idea for the book to Judith Jones who edited, and all the colleagues in the Learning Support Group and Merton schools who contributed to, the Merton version of a SENCO Handbook, produced for their schools.

I also owe a debt to the hundreds of course members from all phases of education, and from most LEAs in the Greater London area, with whom I have worked since 1983. Their projects, on curriculum differentiation and other aspects of whole-school policy development, carried out as part of SENIOS and more recently from the SENCO training modules run from the Institute of Education, have given me in-depth knowledge of how SENCOs manage change. From small beginnings and working within many constraints, these teachers and thousands like them have developed the good practice which benefits children with special educational needs in mainstream schools, much of which is now embodied in the National Standards for SEN Co-ordinators (TTA 1998).

I would also like to thank the following individuals for their constructive criticism and advice about the chapters they read in draft: Hilary Lucus (Harrow), Linda Coventon (LEA Merton Advisor), Janet Warner (Croydon SENCO), Linda Roberts, Christine Clatworthy, Christine Duckworth (members of the Merton LSS), Bernie Marcou (Merton SENCO) and John Brown (Head: Surrey). Also Trevor Cook, Mary Hrekow, Sabina Melidi, Susan Murray, Nick Peacey and Judith Wade, who helped with additional information and advice for the original edition. My thanks also to Zoe Brown, Carol Frankl, Colin Hardy, Jessica Johnson, Mike Murphy, Anne Rawlings and Jim Wight for additional advice for the later editions.

My thanks goes most to my daughter Alison, for her hard work, patience and skill in producing the typed script and for making the production of the book possible. Thanks also to John, my partner, for his patient support and help.

Crown copyright is reproduced with the permission of the Controller of HMSO.

Elizabeth Cowne
February 2003

How to Use this Handbook

This book is intended to help SENCOs, head teachers and governors to implement an effective policy for special educational needs in every school. The following guidance notes on each chapter are to tell you how to find what you need and to link the themes which run through the chapters. The book begins with a debate on issues about SEN and their historic and legislative origins. This could be useful if you wish your staff to look at their concepts of special needs and the value systems of the school. Other staff development activities are all to be found in the Activity Pack at the back of the book.

Chapter 1: Decisions and Dilemmas in SEN: Legislative and Historical Perspectives

The purpose of this chapter is to outline the history of special needs legislation and practice, in order to examine changing perspectives and attitudes left as a legacy from the past.

Chapter 2: Roles and Responsibilities within Whole-school SEN Coordination

This chapter begins by outlining the roles of governors, head, SENCO and class teachers as described in the Code of Practice (2001) and the Disability Rights Commission Code of Practice (2002). The chapter ends by considering how to monitor and evaluate the effectiveness of whole-school policies for SEN. Activities 1, 2 and 6 can be used in conjunction with this topic. Some themes continue in Chapters 9 and 11.

Chapter 3: Identification and Intervention: the Individual Education Plan

This chapter looks at the role of SENCOs in relation to the maintenance of SEN records, the identification of pupils at the school-based stages of the Code of Practice and the subsequent assessment and intervention programmes for all those with IEPs. IEP forms and guidance notes are included in Appendix 3a. Source List 1 gives further information about assessment and further reading. This discussion about the overall management of files and reviews is continued in Chapter 9.

Chapter 4: The Curriculum: Planning for an Inclusive Curriculum

The social nature of learning is discussed, particularly in relation to designing the IEP. Three perspectives on differentiation are then considered: behavioural, cognitive and one which concerns the affective domain. The implications of these perspectives are put into the framework of whole-school curriculum planning.

Chapter 5: The Curriculum: Key Issues for Key Stages

This second chapter on the curriculum gives practical ideas for SENCOs to work with colleagues on differentiation in each of the National Curriculum Key Stages. Activity 3 is a staff development exercise on lesson planning in any of Key Stages 1 to 3. This chapter ends with a discussion about the links between writing IEPs and curriculum planning.

Chapter 6: Managing Effective Support

The theme of roles and responsibilities continues by considering in detail the responsibilities of managing support staff, a role frequently given to SENCOs. Different models of support are described: support for the child, the teacher, the curriculum and the family, to which is added support for the SENCO. Activity 4 can be used for provision planning and Activity 5 to review support policies.

Chapter 7: Multi-professional Networks

This chapter looks at one of the key roles of SENCOs: to build relationships with outside services and agencies, other schools and the networks of voluntary organisations.

Chapter 8: Working in Partnership at Transition Periods

Partnership with other professionals at critical transition points in the pupils' careers is also described: at entry to school, phase transfer, and transition planning at 13+, including transition to further education. Source List 2 contains useful addresses of voluntary organisations.

Chapter 9: Managing Paperwork and Procedures: the Coordinating Role

The bureaucratic role of the SENCO is discussed, including running IEP reviews and annual reviews for those with statements. This chapter is concerned mainly about the SENCO's role, at *School Action Plus* level and when making applications for multi-professional assessments. It is also about other quasi-legal aspects, such as the SENDIST Tribunal and Ofsted inspections. It should be read in conjunction with Chapter 3. Activity 6 is designed to help set success criteria for future targets on policies and practice.

Chapter 10: Working with People: the Consultative Role

This chapter considers three aspects of the SENCO's role: working with children, parents and teachers, and makes links to the roles discussed in other chapters. Appendix 10 contains notes on observation methods and other ideas for understanding the pupil's perspective.

Chapter 11: Working Together towards Inclusive Practice

This final chapter considers the SENCO's role as an agent of change – looking towards inclusive practice. The part that practitioner research plays in this process is also discussed.

CHAPTER 1

Decisions and Dilemmas in Special Educational Needs: Legislative and Historical Perspectives

This chapter begins by exploring some of the historical background of special education in England and Wales and examines changes in attitudes and terminology towards children with a range of disabilities and learning difficulties.

The first hundred years of compulsory schooling began in 1870 with the Elementary Education Act. In the decades which followed, pressure grew from school boards and voluntary groups, to provide a separate system for educating pupils with disabilities. Children with disabilities were seen as unfit for the large classes of 50 or more taught by teachers with no specialist training. The usual solution was to segregate these children into a special school. Funds to run these often came from charities. By 1918 some school boards in metropolitan areas were educating the 'unfit' in special classes within normal schools. Others with disabilities were provided for by a mixture of institutions or by home visiting. The voluntary charitable societies developed a professional expertise in offering vocational training as well as care for particular groups, such as the blind and the deaf.

Special education had higher costs, so only some school boards offered provision in classes or special schools. Rural communities often kept their disabled pupils within their normal schools or gave no schooling at all. Universal access to education for all children with disabilities was to come later. This segregation and isolation often meant that disabled children were denied access to the normal activities and opportunities of the local school and community. In some cases where the disabled child did attend a village school their needs may not have been understood and they often suffered ridicule.

The 1944 Act

At the end of the Second World War, the 1944 Act was passed. The policy behind this Act was to provide statutory education at primary and secondary stages to all children, including those with disabilities. The only exceptions were those who had a severe mental handicap, for whom it took a further 26 years and new legislation to give Education Authorities the responsibility for their education. The 1944 Act stated that LEAs should

> secure that provision is made for pupils who suffer from any disability of mind or body, by providing either in special schools or otherwise, special educational treatment, that is to say education by special methods for persons suffering from that disability.

The LEA was to ascertain which children needed special treatment and then decide on placement according to category. The advice used to make this decision came largely from medical officers. Later, psychologists began to be employed to test this group of children and to assist the medical officers in their decision-making. Tomlinson (1982) remarks that

> The history of special education must be viewed in terms of the benefits it brought for a developing industrial society, the benefits for the normal mass education system of a special sub-system of education and the benefits that medical, psychological, educational personnel derive from encouraging new areas of professional expertise.

Towards the end of the period 1944–78 much had changed. A complex special education system of schools, classes and services had been built up. Teacher training in SEN specialisms had developed. Children with severe learning difficulties were at last given the right to education through the Handicapped Children Act (1970). Parents had begun, through voluntary groups, to exert pressure for change. Influences from abroad (the USA in particular) were affecting the thinking of such groups. The Warnock Committee, set up in 1974, produced a report in 1978. From this grew the most significant legislation for special education – the 1981 Act.

The 1981 Act

The 1981 Act redefined the population of pupils with disabilities as those with 'special educational needs'. This Act gave clear guidelines about assessment procedures and the issuing of a statement of special educational needs. Statements are documents which summarise a pupil's learning difficulties and list suitable provision. Building on the recommendations of the Warnock report much was said in the 1981 Act about involving parents in decision-making in relation to assessment. Schools were also given responsibilities to identify the full range of those with SEN using the five-stage assessment procedure suggested in the Warnock report.

The term 'special educational needs' depends not only on a concept of discontinuity of provision, but also on the concept of relativity of need. This is the most fundamental dilemma of special educational needs, because although the term includes children with disabilities, it also includes those whose educational progress in learning is significantly slower than that of their peer group, for whatever cause. To identify which individuals have such needs and so require something extra or something different from what is normally provided requires a decision-making process.

The 1981 Act embodied much of what had been developing over time and could be perceived as building on 'best practice'. The Act influenced attitudes of teachers in mainstream schools. They began to recognise that pupils with SEN were their responsibility. Integration policies were adopted by many schools and LEAs. Training for special educational needs in ordinary schools (SENIOS) was funded through training grants from 1983 onwards (DES Circulars 3/83–5/85). Those responsible for special needs work were not at this time called special educational needs coordinators. This responsibility was often taken by either a member of the senior management team or was in the hands of the 'remedial' teacher or team.

Between 1983 and 1994 the role of the SENCO became fully established and a description of the role was written into the Code of Practice (DfE 1994a). In 1998 the Teacher Training Agency (TTA) published the *National Standards for Special Educational Needs Co-ordinators*. These set out the core purposes of the role of the SENCO and the key outcomes of SEN coordination. These standards enhance the role of the SENCO, bringing it into higher profile. They are also being used as guidelines for SENCO training courses.

Multi-professional decision-making

The more complex a child's need, the more people will be involved in the decision-making process within and across organisations and professions. Communication between these individuals and organisations is important if coherent and consistent decisions are to be made. The power base of those who make such decisions has changed across the century. In the earliest decades, the medical profession, often alone, chose which child went to a special school or indeed had any schooling at all. The LEA was intended to ascertain which children needed special treatment and decide on placement according to category, but the advice used to make this decision came largely from medical officers (see Appendix 1). Sutton (1982) states that:

> For years, it remained unclear who were the gate keepers to special education and despite the law's clear statement that the final decision lay with the LEA, in practice the actual decision very often lay with a medical officer following prescribed procedures. (p. 11)

The 1981 Act attached great value to multi-disciplinary assessment. The power of the medical profession and its model, which had affected special education for so long, was reduced. The focus was on educational needs and these were to be described in educational terms and met by educational provision. Treatment was not a word used in describing this provision. Guidance on assessment and statements was given through Circular 1/83.

The 1981 Act required joint decision-making between health, education and social services. Parents began to have more say in their child's assessment and voluntary organisations began to lobby on behalf of different groups of children.

Provision is made across what Fish (1989) called dimensions of need, all of which lie on a continuum. Decision-making becomes complex when the providers of different resources have different priorities. Education, for example, may specify that health authorities should provide therapies for children with SEN, but the health authority may not see this as a priority area for their resources. This is a further dilemma which arises between cross-professional provision: one which must be resolved on a regional or national level.

The Education Reform Act (1988)

The Education Reform Act (1988) also contributed to the thinking about pupils with learning difficulties. This Act states that all children have a right to a 'broad, balanced, relevant and differentiated curriculum'. On the positive side this meant all pupils now had an 'entitlement curriculum'. On the negative side teachers were overloaded by the requirement to teach the number of subjects specified and to test and assess pupils' progress in all of these subjects. Schools began to be more aware of their overall performance as judged by these tests. Pupils with special educational needs were not always seen as an asset when comparative tables of results were produced. Local management of schools (LMS) meant that money followed pupils and the school roll defined the overall resources available. Special needs pupils might use more of these resources than the school wished.

Levels of resourcing

Extra resourcing for special educational needs makes assumptions about what constitutes normal provision across schools or local authorities. Since the Education Reform Act, which introduced LMS, schools have had different levels of resourcing. Schools also differ in the amounts they allocate to their special educational needs budget. Schools are required to allocate funds between and amongst their pupils with special educational needs in an equitable manner.

As well as a discontinuity principle in special educational needs, there is also a continuity of need between what is perceived as special or normal. The graduation

3

is such that the cut-off point can be arbitrary, or appear so. The decision as to where to draw this line is made by a range of individuals and organisations. All of these have differing perspectives about their priorities, which depend on their knowledge and their value systems. This presents another dilemma of special educational needs. Different groups may have different constructs of the term 'special educational needs', which then relate to different priorities about how to use available resources to meet these needs.

One way in which schools attempt to meet the additional needs of certain pupils is to request a multi-professional assessment by the LEA. This could result in a statement, which should bring extra resources to the school. The problem arises when too many pupils' needs are met through the statementing process as this can discourage schools from developing effective or inclusive policies.

The Children Act (1989)

This Act, though not focused on education, was influential in changing viewpoints about children's rights and parental responsibilities. It also influenced thinking about these rights within the 1993 Education Act and the Code of Practice. The Code of Practice (DfES 2001b) has a whole chapter on pupil participation. This chapter states very clearly that all children and young people have rights. This includes being involved in making decisions and exercising choices.

The 1993 Act and Code of Practice (1994)

The 1993 Education Act (Part 3) replaced much of the 1981 legislation without significant changes. The new elements were the setting up of the SEN tribunal and the publishing of the *Code of Practice on the Identification and Assessment of Special Educational Needs* (DfE 1994a). This document has a status between a regulation, which is mandatory, and a circular, which is advisory. Schools and LEAs are required to use their best endeavours to 'have regard to' the requirements of the Code of Practice to make provision for pupils with SEN. However, certain parts are mandatory.

The 1993 Act and Code of Practice (1994) pushed the decision-making surrounding statement and provision further towards schools and parents, but final decisions were still made by the LEAs, who took advice from other professionals through the multi-disciplinary assessment. Parents can and do initiate requests for assessment and have an increasing amount of power when exercised through the SEN tribunal. The number of cases going to tribunal has risen continually since it was set up, although there is concern that litigation is not the most effective or efficient way to resolve disputes. The 1996 Act replaced that of 1993, consolidating various pieces of legislation, but not making major changes in relation to SEN.

National Curriculum Revisions

In 1994 the Dearing Revision of the National Curriculum was issued. This was an attempt to 'slim down' the original orders and to lighten the load for teachers. Guidance documents were issued which gave schools more flexibility in planning the curriculum and suggested that the school's population be considered in some detail when planning schemes of work. Special arrangements were put in place to vary assessments for pupils with statements.

But during the same period, secondary schools were required to publish their exam results and these could be compared through league tables in the local and national press. League tables are now also published for KS2 English and mathematics results. In 1998 the National Frameworks for Literacy and Numeracy were drawn up and these strategies are now in place in all primary schools – now also to be extended to KS3. However, these initiatives do not always give sufficient attention to the needs of those with disabilities or learning difficulties.

The National Curriculum (1999)

The National Curriculum was revised again at the end of 1999. The intention was that the need to disapply pupils from the National Curriculum should be kept to a minimum. The document explains in detail how principles of inclusion can be put into practice. The Inclusion Statement reminds us that schools have the responsibility to provide a broad and balanced curriculum for all pupils. The document sets out three principles underlying the more inclusive curriculum, also giving examples to illustrate how this can be done.

Code of Practice (2001)

The Code of Practice (2001) is differently structured to make it more accessible to readers. It also includes new chapters which emphasise the importance of working in partnership with parents and listening to pupils' views.

The sections on Identification and Assessment are presented for three phases: early education settings, primary and secondary phases. The staged assessment procedure is simplified and called a graduated response. The school-based stages are now called *School Action* and *School Action Plus*. Interventions should be recorded on IEPs for pupils at these stages and for those with statements of SEN. The last chapter of the Code of Practice (2001) describes the working partnership between agencies. The *SEN Toolkit* (DfES 2001c) was published at the same time as the Code to give practical advice.

Devolution of funding

There has also been further pressure from government policy about how much of the education resource can be kept by the LEAs for central administration. One effect of this has been that LEAs have devolved as much money as possible directly to school budgets. This often now includes money which in the past paid for central support services to assess and teach pupils with SEN. There continues to be a decline in the size of support services for pupils both with and without a statement of SEN. Schools choose how devolved and delegated funds are used and may buy back from central services if these are available. School governors are required to develop and publish a policy which shows how resources for SEN are used 'between and amongst' pupils with SEN. Only some LEAs have developed good monitoring systems to ensure that pupils' needs are indeed met by the delegated resources intended for that purpose.

Flexible resource management

At the time of the 1981 Act, Statements were seen as being for those children with quite exceptional and complex needs. Over the last decade in particular the trend in statementing has been to increase the percentage from under 2 per cent to over 3 per cent of the school population in many LEAs. The process of issuing statements is costly, so although the outcome is usually valued by parents, LEAs try to limit the number of multi-professional assessments to those who they consider are in greatest need. Another way of resourcing is by devolving most funds to schools so they can provide for additional needs that have been assessed and recorded for groups. Nevertheless every LEA still has to be able to look after some children with complex needs.

Within the organisation of a school or LEA there must be decision-making processes for identifying and assessing needs. This requires policies on how such needs are to be met, what provision will be made and who manages, monitors and reviews this provision. Priorities may change and, depending on how flexible the system, resources may be reallocated. Resources are finite, however large or small, so decisions about priorities are essential. If resources are tied up with individuals in an inflexible way they cannot easily be reallocated when the need arises. Resources tied into statements of SEN remain static and flexibility may be lost. This argument might be extended to the debates about special school provision but the status quo is difficult to change.

Research on the 1994 Code of Practice

Since the publication of the Code of Practice (1994) there have been three follow-up Ofsted surveys assessing how it has been working in practice and summarising recommendations for future development (Ofsted 1996b, 1997, 1999). These reports all showed that progress had been made in:

- giving pupils increased access to a broad and balanced curriculum;
- successfully identifying pupils' learning and behavioural needs and being successful in keeping up SEN registers and preparing IEPs;
- putting SEN policies in place, though many do not fully fulfil all legal requirements.

All reports gave indications of the aspects of work still to be done in many schools. This is a whole-school issue – one that requires strategic planning as part of the schools' overall Improvement Plan and links to other school policies. Schools are at different stages in developing their policy and practice, so it is important to take stock of where your school is along this path.

Inclusive school systems

Schools can be defined as open systems, which include parents and communities as part of the system. Some schools can include more of their community within the school than others. This depends on the knowledge, competence and confidence of staff and on effective policies of support and communication. It also depends on the value-system of the governors and senior management team and how these pervade the whole school. It is said that a school that is effective for pupils with SEN is usually effective for all pupils. Such a school will support staff and parents' needs as well as those of the pupils. It will run efficiently and standards and expectations will be high. Such a school is likely to have a more inclusive policy for pupils with problems or differences.

One of the regulations which was brought into being at the time of the Code of Practice (1994) stated that governing bodies of all county schools are required to publish information about their SEN policy. *The SENCO Guide* (DfEE 1997) reminds SENCOs that this policy should reflect the practice and aspirations of the whole school and be accessible to the whole school community. Schools are also bound in law to report annually to parents on the working of their SEN policies. The Index for Inclusion (Booth et al. 2000) was published and the government sent a copy to every school. Its purpose was to offer a tool to schools and LEAs to audit their whole-school policy and practice in relation to inclusion. The theme of inclusion continues in Chapter 11.

The purpose of this book is to support the SENCO, head teachers, governors, staff and parents by outlining the key aspects of whole-school SEN policy development and to provide help in reviewing progress. Each school will need to make its own decisions about the SEN dilemmas and how to resolve them in relation to local priorities and resources. When reviewing the school's SEN policy and practice it may be useful to begin by reflecting on the changes in perspective about children with disabilities that have been described in this chapter. Some questions to ask might be:

- How have the legacies of the past affected our present concepts of special educational needs and disability?
- How important is the language used to describe pupils' difficulties?
- How has power in decision-making changed over the years in relation to pupils with SEN? Who has the greatest power now?
- How have parent and pupil rights changed?
- What changes have been seen in your own school, over the last ten years, in relation to SEN provision and practice?

CHAPTER 2

Roles and Responsibilities within Whole-school SEN Coordination

This chapter introduces the theme of roles and responsibilities in mainstream schools for pupils with special educational needs. This includes the roles and responsibilities of the governors and head teacher, as well as those of the SENCO. It is important to conceptualise these as part of a whole-school approach to SEN coordination. The overall responsibilities lie with the governing body and the head teacher, who carry out the strategic planning for the school's development. All teachers have a responsibility for those pupils in their classes with special educational needs. Parents, pupils and ancillary staff also have their parts to play. The coordination of the day-to-day policy and practice for SEN is the responsibility of the SENCO. As everyone has a role to play, this means it is necessary to have a whole-school approach to the management of SEN.

Effective schools manage special educational needs by being clear about their priorities when allocating roles and responsibilities. Effective school policies also depend on good communication systems between all those holding these responsibilities. The school moves forward in its development by integrating special needs policies into the School Improvement Plan as a whole. Often what is good practice for SEN is good practice for all. Effective schools remain so by being reflective organisations which manage change. This requires a mixture of flexibility and consistency. The challenge of SEN is that of constant change and the need to adapt not only to the demands of the pupils but also to new legislation or ways of allocating resources.

The Code of Practice (1994) described the roles and responsibilities for SEN in a mainstream school. The duties of the governing body are given in Section 317A of the Education Act 1996 (see Appendix 2a). All schools must have regard to the Code of Practice when carrying out their duties towards pupils with SEN.

The Code of Practice (2001) has a table (p. 18) showing the roles and responsibilities for everyone working in:

- maintained mainstream schools
- maintained special schools
- early years settings.

The Code advises flexibility and variation in the response adopted by schools and early years settings but reminds everyone that they must be able to demonstrate that in the arrangements made for children with SEN, they are fulfilling their statutory duty to have regard to the Code. 'Ofsted will consider the effectiveness of their policies and practices and the extent to which they have regard to the Code' (Code of Practice 2001, 1:38).

Whatever arrangements are made in a particular school, statutory duties remain with the governing body. The Code of Practice also uses the term 'responsible person'. This is usually the head teacher, but may be a governor, often the chair, unless the governing body have designated another governor. The responsible person must, when informed by the LEA that a pupil has a statement of special educational needs, let *all* in the school who are likely to teach this pupil know of these needs and how they are to be met. The management of this information flow usually falls to the SENCO who must select what is essential for each adult in the system on a 'need to know' basis. The Disability Rights Commission (DRC) Code of Practice (2002) should be given due attention so that all staff are aware of pupils with disabilities and their requirements. Staff will need awareness training about how to avoid discrimination against those with disabilities.

Governors' responsibilities

Under Section 317 of the 1996 Education Act, the governing body of a maintained mainstream school must report annually to parents on their policy for pupils with special educational needs (161.5). The details of information which must be included are given in the 17 points listed in Schedule 1 (Reg. 3(1)) (see Appendix 2b) and explained more fully by Circular 6/94. Governors must also be able to show how resources for SEN have been allocated *to and among* children with special educational needs.

The SENCO Guide (DfEE 1997) recommends that school policies should be specific about how much money was allocated for SEN provision and how it was spent. Such openness, the Guide suggests, will ensure that limited resources are spent to maximum effect. The Guide further suggests that it may be useful to establish a policy review team which includes representatives from the teaching staff, governing body and parents.

School responsibilities under the Disability Discrimination Act (1995) Part 4

Another Code of Practice for schools, related to the Disability Discrimination Act, came into operation in September 2002. This Code explains the responsibilities of schools relating to the Special Education and Disability Act (2001). It is advisory but it may be referred to in legal proceedings as the Special Educational Needs and Disability Tribunal (SENDIST). Schools must not discriminate against disabled pupils by treating them less favourably or by putting them at a disadvantage. This means that school planning and policies should address three distinct elements:

- improvements in access to the curriculum;
- physical improvements to increase access to education and associated services;
- improvements in the provision of information in a range of formats for disabled pupils.

The DRC *Code of Practice for Schools* (DRC 2002a) gives practical advice on how to avoid discrimination against disabled pupils and prospective disabled pupils. The examples relate to aspects of school education that are covered by Part 4 of the Act, namely admissions, education and associated services and exclusions. This Act and Code apply to all schools in England, Scotland and Wales including independent and publicly funded mainstream nursery, primary, secondary, and special schools.

> The duty on schools to make reasonable adjustments is anticipatory. It is the potential for a substantial disadvantage that should trigger a consideration of what reasonable steps might need to be taken. Schools cannot, in general, wait until a disabled pupil has arrived before making reasonable adjustments. This may be too late and it may not be possible to take reasonable steps before the pupil is placed at a substantial disadvantage. (DRC *Code of Practice for Schools* 2002, 6:12)

> The reasonable adjustments duty is owed to disabled children in general, not simply to individual disabled children. (DRC *Code of Practice for Schools* 2002, 6:13)

The implications of this Act and its Code are clear: in future schools must develop policy and practice which will prevent unlawful or discriminatory practice. This is a whole-institution issue and one to which the SENCO can contribute. However, SENCOs cannot be held individually responsible for school policy and practice.

The role of the Special Educational Needs Coordinator

Governors or head teachers might be led to think that a school's SENCO could look after all aspects of the school's special needs practice and the new disability policies. However, this is not a feasible option in any but very small schools, where the role may be held by the head teacher. This area is too broad and too pervasive of the curriculum and ethos of a school to be any one person's sole responsibility.

The role of the SENCO and the concept of a whole-school policy for special educational needs has been developing over the years since 1983. All maintained schools now accept in principle that they have responsibilities for special needs and that someone has to be named as their SENCO, even though that role may well be doubled and trebled with other roles held by that person. Independent schools are also becoming more aware of these responsibilities and many are appointing SENCOs and developing SEN policies.

Managing and training staff

The Code of Practice (2001) states that the responsibilities of a SENCO will include:

- overseeing the day-to-day operation of the school's SEN policy
- co-ordinating provision for children with special educational needs
- liaising with and advising fellow teachers
- managing learning support assistants
- overseeing the records of all children with special educational needs
- liaising with parents of children with special educational needs
- contributing to the in-service training of staff
- liaising with external agencies including the LEA's support and educational psychology services, health and social services, and voluntary bodies.

One aspect of the SENCO role which has developed and is now fully recognised in the Code of Practice (2001) is that of managing and training support staff. Over the last decade there has been a large increase in the number of additional staff working in schools (see Chapter 6). *The National Standards for SENCOs* states that SENCOs should take an active part in leading and managing staff. Specifically they should:

> Advise, contribute to and, where appropriate, co-ordinate the professional development of staff to increase their effectiveness in responding to pupils with SEN, and provide support and training to trainee and newly qualified teachers in relation to the standards for the award of Qualified Teacher Status, Career Entry Profiles and standards for induction. (TTA 1998, p. 13)

Time as a resource

In primary schools many SENCOs are also full-time class teachers or hold other responsibility posts. In secondary schools the SENCO may head the SEN department or be a subject teacher for part of the time. There is clearly a need to *select* from the above list according to time and expertise available. Of vital importance is communication between all parts of the system. It is helpful if

SENCOs can be part of the senior management team. The head teacher should allocate time for liaison and planning among everyone involved and for the SENCO to see parents. The policy must make it clear who is responsible for each aspect of the work. The referral and information systems of the school should also be clear to all users, including the parents.

The Code of Practice (2001) suggests that the role of the SENCO is at least equivalent to a curriculum coordinator in a primary school or a head of year or the head of department in a secondary school. The Code says that: 'Governing bodies and head teachers will need to give careful thought to the SENCO's timetable in the light of the Code and in the context of the resources available to the school' (5:10).

There is clearly a need to relate all of these roles to the resources of time and expertise available among the *whole* teaching staff. In larger schools, the work should be shared amongst relevant staff. These could include the head, deputy, class teacher, subject coordinator or year head. A time budget needs to be worked out to see what time is available and to match this with a prioritised list of tasks and roles (see Activity 1 in the Activity Pack). When carrying out this exercise try to see SEN coordination as a whole-school issue. While some of those with responsibility will be involved in a **strategic** role (that is, they will need to make decisions relating to policy and resources), others may only need **information** about activities. Some tasks will require **action** to be taken by one or more members of staff. Begin by taking an audit of how staff perceive the tasks and roles which might be necessary. Who will take responsibility for strategic planning? Who will take the action? Who needs or gives information? (See Activity 1.)

Developing and maintaining a whole-school approach

Developing these roles and coordinating the whole-school approach will evolve over time. Schools will be at different stages of development in this process, therefore it is important to evaluate what your school has achieved. The next step may be to check staff understanding and knowledge of your existing school SEN policy and evaluate what each believes

(a) *should* be the policy
(b) is *actually* the case at present (see Activity 2).

The gaps between the scores of these two lines should be examined and priority areas for development chosen by analysis of the data. Schools may well have policies on paper, but it is the improvement of *all* pupils' learning over time which will be the acid test. For example, do the policies lead to good record-keeping, open communication between school and parents and effective use of support? Policy means intended action. But it is based on a value system which may mean changing the attitudes of some or all staff, and such change takes time. The SENCO may be a catalyst for change, but change cannot be expected without the full support of the head teacher. Each year, the policy must be evaluated against the success criteria of the previous year (see Figure 2.1).

Monitoring and evaluation

Part of SEN coordination is the monitoring and evaluation on a regular basis of the school's SEN policy and practice. Monitoring may be led by the SENCO or by members of the senior management team (SMT). If targets in the previous year have been set using success criteria and clear performance indicators then it will be easy to see what has been achieved. It is important, therefore, when choosing targets as part of the school's Improvement Plan to:

(a) make these small and precise enough to be achieved
(b) set criteria or indicators so that success can be recorded or lack of success investigated

(c) allocate roles and responsibilities for the implementation of the target;
(d) set a time-scale on implementation;
(e) evaluate how successful the school was in reaching this target.

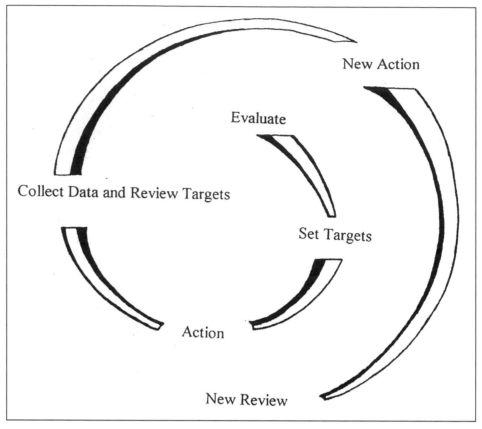

Figure 2.1 Review cycle

This means that at the end of each year the policy must be evaluated and new targets decided for the following year along with some new success criteria. The review needs to ask:

- Were last year's targets reached?
- Have changes to provision or policy been made?
- Have any roles and responsibilities changed significantly or new people been appointed?
- Has the LEA policy changed in any way which will influence school policy? (for example, have SEN funding arrangements changed?)

(See Activity 6 for practice in setting success criteria for a target area of policy.)

Developments and changes in the school's policy and practice must be made known to the governing body by the head teacher or SENCO, and the governors must include this information in their annual report to parents. If the policy is to remain active and dynamic, it must be seen as a **process** of development. This requires maximum involvement of the head teacher and senior management team, representation from the curriculum and pastoral systems, as well as the co-ordination of practice by the SENCO. If effective, the whole-school policy is likely to enhance the teaching, learning and well-being of *all* pupils. The SEN policy needs to be seen as part of the School's Improvement Plan (SIP) and to link with other existing policies such as those for equal opportunities or behaviour. There should also be a strong relationship to the assessment policy and to curriculum planning.

> Regulations made under Section 42 of the School Standards and Framework Act 1998 require that the governing body's annual report **must** include information on the implementation of the governing body's policy on pupils with special educational needs and any changes to the policy during the last year.
> (Code of Practice 2001, 1:28)

The SEN budget

Schools have additional funding allocated to them under the LMS scheme for SEN. This may be given in relation to a variety of indicators, of which the most common is the number of pupils who are eligible for free school meals. In some LEAs funding for pupils with statements has also been delegated. Schools are accountable for the proper use of all these funds. This means senior management and governors should set a SEN budget and make it known how resources have been allocated *between and amongst* all those identified as having SEN. It is up to the school to decide how it will apportion all funds except those earmarked for statements. It may use money from its general age/pupil weighted funding (APWU) as well as money in the additional needs funds. Special needs activities are often time consuming so this should be taken into account when the school sets its SEN budget and when the targets are set to develop the policy and practice for the next year. The SENCO must be fully aware of these funding arrangements and any procedures put in place to monitor them, either by the school or the LEA.

> The National Standards for SENCOs states clearly that SENCOs identify with the support of the head teacher and governing body, appropriate resources to support the teaching of pupils with SEN and monitor their use in terms of efficiency, effectiveness and safety. (TTA 1998, p. 14)

However, experience shows that many SENCOs do not feel empowered to become involved in policy and resourcing issues. They may not have access to information or feel they can ask for it. In these cases, the strategic SEN coordination is in the hands of the head and governors. It will be important for the SENCO to ensure that the head teacher and governing body have up-to-date information about the numbers of pupils at each of the school-based stages of the Code or those with statements of SEN. This is because this will have implications for resourcing and use of funds. Provision mapping (Activity 4 and as described in Chapter 6) could also be helpful in monitoring the SEN budget.

CHAPTER 3

Identification and Intervention: the Individual Education Plan

Keeping SEN records

The starting point of all work in SEN is the identification of pupils who may have learning difficulties of a significant nature. Schools' assessment policies should include the procedures for identifying those pupils considered to have additional or different needs. These pupils' needs will be met through the graduated response as given in the Code of Practice (2001). These children will have Individual Education Plans (IEPs) which require regular reviewing and monitoring (see Appendix 3a). This review process is the key to successful SEN management. Once a pupil has been identified, information gathering and assessment take place, and this contributes to a planned intervention aimed at reducing the pupil's learning difficulties and increasing their access to the curriculum. SENCOs have a major role in advising and supporting staff over such planning.

The Code of Practice (2001) regulations state that the SEN policy must explain the school's identification, assessment, monitoring and review procedures, including the graduated assessment procedures. Those with statements for SEN for whom the school is responsible must have annual reviews. Decisions about which children have sufficient or appropriate needs to require an IEP must be managed, usually by the SENCO. While all children have individual needs, these are not necessarily related to learning difficulties or disabilities as defined by the 1981 or 1996 Acts.

To warrant a description of SEN a child will have learning difficulties which cause concern over time, probably to both parents and teachers. Such a child is not responding as expected to the curriculum on offer or cannot cope within the normal classroom environment without additional help. The Code of Practice encourages all class teachers to raise any concerns they may have, usually with the SENCO. However, certain decisions may seem to be difficult to make.

English as an additional language

Children for whom English is not their first language may still be developing their bilingual ability. At the early stages of this process, access to the curriculum, as delivered, is difficult. These children do not necessarily have learning difficulties, indeed they may be very efficient learners. If these learners are at the early stages of learning English they should *not* be considered as having SEN. Hall (2001) writes:

> Some pupils whose first language is not English will need support to extend their speaking and writing repertoires and to practise new words and phrases in a relevant context. Schools must however ensure that lack of English proficiency is not assumed to indicate SEN or learning difficulties. (p. 78)

The Code of Practice (2001) states:

> Lack of competence in English must not be equated with learning difficulties. At the same time, when children who have English as an additional language make slow progress, it should not be assumed that their language status is the only reason; they may have learning difficulties. (Code of Practice, 5:16)

Speaking to the child's parents is advisable, in order to understand their perception of the child's progress. It will be important to find out how long the child has been learning English and how the child functions using their home language. It may be possible to arrange assessment in the child's own language through local services. Pupils should be encouraged to use their own language as well as English (see Appendix 3b for checklist).

Able pupils

Able or gifted pupils need a differentiated curriculum. They need to be identified and their needs should be met by providing opportunities for extension and problem-solving, and a challenging delivery of the curriculum. Schools should have a separate policy for able and gifted pupils, and curriculum planning which takes account of such pupils. They do *not* however have learning difficulties and should *not* be seen as having SEN. Again, there may be gifted children who have other problems or disabilities. In these cases there will be other reasons for considering their needs for monitoring and further assessment. This is particularly the case when performance changes and is not what was previously expected. George (1997) states that some gifted children show themselves as very able by their high energy level and intense curiosity, others are more difficult to spot and deliberately hide their talents.

Collating information about the child when concerns are first noted

All information about concerns should be collected and collated. Parents' views and the child's own perception, as well as evidence from previous records, are included in this collection of concerns. Observation of the child within the class situation may reveal contextual reasons for the difficulty. It is important not to adopt a totally 'within child' model of SEN. Learning difficulties can develop through the way schools function. Relationships within school need to be examined, between child and teacher and child and other children.

The majority of pupils can have their needs met by a careful process of assessment and planning. Schools now carry out a great deal of assessment within the National Curriculum arrangements. The Programmes of Study help teachers to structure their teaching by progression through a planned curriculum. This has both advantages and disadvantages for SEN, which will be further explored in Chapters 4 and 5. The next step is to carry out any further assessments which seem necessary to answer questions raised by this initial investigation.

Assessment: tools and testing

The Task Group for Assessment and Testing, when planning the first steps of the National Curriculum assessment, stated that:

> Promoting children's learning is a principal aim of schools. Assessment lies at the heart of this process. The assessment process itself should not determine what is taught and learned. It should be the servant not the master of the curriculum. It should be an integral part of the educational process continually providing both 'feedback' and 'feed forward'. (DES 1987, Paras 3, 4)

Assessment for SEN should therefore be seen as part of the school's assessment policy and not as an additional 'bolt on' process. One of the important conclusions of the Ofsted 1999 review of the Code of Practice was that:

> IEPs are most likely to be effective when they operate within a culture of effective and detailed educational planning. They are unlikely to be effective if they are not part of the school's overall arrangements for assessment and recording. (Ofsted 1999, p. 22)

A full survey of assessment tools and concepts is outside the scope of this book. The following section highlights certain priorities about identification and assessment that usually concern teachers at each of the Key Stages.

Early years settings

Children thought to have SEN in nursery and reception classes may either be identified at entry to school or their needs may emerge over time. Teachers are sometimes reluctant to use the label SEN, because children develop at such varying rates and do so unevenly across different aspects of development, e.g. language, socialisation and cognitive functions. It is therefore very important to keep careful records of pupils and record any notable differences in development.

The key to good identification in the early years is careful observation. Teachers and helpers need training in accurate observation. They also need help in keeping purposeful records. Such records could form the basis of any decisions about SEN.

Early years practitioners have a key role to play in working with parents to identify learning needs and to develop an effective strategy to meet these needs using IEPs if appropriate.

The Code of Practice (2001) has a chapter on Early Years settings. This includes a version of the graduated response to identification and provision. Liaison with parents and other professionals, often from the health service, is a key role for Early Years SENCOs, as is careful record keeping.

Those who may require additional or different provision might include a child who:

- makes little or no progress even when teaching approaches are particularly targeted to improve the child's identified area of weakness
- continues working at levels significantly below those expected for children of a similar age in certain areas
- presents persistent emotional and/or behavioural difficulties, which are not ameliorated by the behaviour management techniques usually employed in the setting
- has sensory or physical problems, and continues to make little or no progress despite the provision of personal aids and equipment
- has communication and/or interaction difficulties, and requires specific individual interventions in order to access learning.

(see Code of Practice 4:21)

These children should have IEPs written for them and regularly reviewed. Outside agency support may be requested for those who continue to make little progress and whose parents are concerned. A few children will have significant needs which cause concern and for these a request for a statutory assessment may be made to the LEA. LEAs will use reports from those professionals most closely involved with the child in their decision-making process.

Key Stage 1: assessment for SEN

The National Curriculum teacher-based assessments at Key Stage 1 are largely based on observation, although there are standard tasks which form the basis of Standard Assessment Tests (SATs) at the end of Key Stage 1. However, it is important to look at the 'whole child' when making additional assessments. The Foundation Curriculum (QCA 2000) will be of help in choosing a range of appropriate developmental areas to observe and note. It is very important to remember that young children develop at different rates. A slow start in one area may not indicate a special educational need. The child may just need more time and more experience to develop this area.

Most schools use teacher-based, criterion-referenced assessment as a normal method of both screening for pupils with problems and planning interventions. This type of assessment watches the process of learning and notes what the child *can* do as a baseline. This is used to plan the next steps. A further refinement of this is objective-based assessment leading to target-setting on IEPs. The 'Portage' scheme, working with parents of pre-school children with severe difficulties and disabilities, also approaches intervention through the test-teach-test cycle. These approaches stem from earlier work in special schools, and the behaviourist approach of applied behaviour analysis (see Chapter 4).

The principle of these approaches is to work from what the child *can already do* to the *objective* of the next priority goal. Each task is split into steps. This process is known as task analysis. A specific *criterion* for success must be stated in advance, as must the *conditions* under which the task will be achieved.

Such an approach is ideal for ensuring progress for some pupils with SEN. Often, just defining the objective is sufficient to solve the problem. Once teacher and child agree on the goal, in many cases success is almost instant. Observations of how the child learns will also be made during this test-teach-test cycle. What strategies are particularly successful? What learning styles does the child use? What support level is required? These observations help when planning an IEP for those pupils for whom *School Action* is seen as appropriate.

Using the P scales

Children whose development is delayed may not make sufficient progress to register on the National Curriculum levels and be given a 'W' to show they are working towards Level One. For such children the newly developed P Scales will be a valuable way to address slow progress (QCA 2001). Evidence of participation may be collected through annotated photographs as shown in Buck and Davis (2001).

Key Stage 2: assessment for SEN

Since the National Literacy and Numeracy Strategies were established, identifying children with learning difficulties has focused attention on these aspects of the curriculum. Additional Literacy Strategies have now also been introduced to help those who are moving at a slower pace. These strategies should reduce the number of pupils with reading, writing and mathematical problems. However there may still be some who require careful teaching which takes account of individual difficulties in acquiring fluency and confidence in reading and writing. A group IEP may be a useful way to record the needs of such pupils in an economical way.

It is also important not to miss children whose needs may be less obvious, for example quiet children who may be overlooked in favour of those whose behaviour is boisterous. These children may be lacking in confidence, have language or communication difficulties or general learning problems.

There are two ways commonly used to screen the pupil population in the junior years. One is to use a checklist about observed learning, noting learning styles and attitudes which may be an important clue to effective intervention. The other is to use standardised tests of reading, spelling and mathematics, but teacher-based, criterion-referenced assessment should also continue to play an important part in identifying effective strategies for intervention.

Published test material

Published tests and diagnostic materials can be useful to an experienced user for establishing standards in reading and spelling in particular. It is very important to familiarise yourself with the test manuals to establish fitness of purpose. You should check:

- the age range the test is designed for;
- the date of publication and the population on which it was normed (i.e. is it out of date? Or inappropriate for your class?);
- the precise instructions for giving tests to individuals or groups.

These are particularly important if a reliable, standardised score is to be achieved. There are also a range of texts to establish the level of phonological awareness achieved by those with reading difficulties (see Source List 1).

Miscue analysis

Diagnostic tests can be useful in sorting out baseline information for skills such as reading, spelling and mathematics. The purpose of all assessment must be to lead to appropriate curriculum and lesson planning. Caution needs to be taken about the overuse of normative information from test results. It may be more useful to see *how* a child reads a text, and note his or her strategies. One way to do this is to use a miscue analysis. The child is given a text of about 100 words from a book, which you think is approximately correct for his or her reading ability. You ask the child to read it aloud and say you will not be helping out on hard words. It is best to have a tape recorder running so that you can analyse the reading thoroughly. You should have a prepared sheet of the text on which to mark the types of omissions and mistakes. You should encourage the child to read but not supply missing words unless the child is showing distress. If the text is too hard, stop the test and do it another day with a simpler text. You should mark all the misreadings, omissions, refusals and self-corrections. This will tell you about the child's reading strategies and give you an indicator of whether the text can be read independently or only with instruction. If less than 90 per cent of the words have been read correctly, the text is only being read at a frustration level and is too hard. A text which is being read at instructional level will have less than 5 per cent of the words read incorrectly or left unread. It is important not to let children read at frustration level on a regular basis.

Children with emotional and behavioural difficulties

Some pupils' difficulties in learning are caused by their emotional state or by their inability to learn appropriate behaviour. Pupils may be continually off-task, sometimes disrupting others, sometimes themselves. Such pupils often have low self-esteem and poor learning. Good record-keeping for pupils with emotional or behavioural difficulties will note:

- information about the pupil's learning style;
- relationships with peers and adults;
- relevant information from parents about the pupil in the home context;
- the pupil's attitudes to learning (can they risk failure?);
- observation about the pupil's strengths which can be used to build better self-esteem;
- how this pupil can be helped to function more effectively within the class.

General principles relating assessment to planning

All assessment must provide the detail needed to plan to match the next step or next experience for the group in question. The total learning context for the pupil must be taken into account. This includes noting relationships with parents and teachers and features related to home environments. It is very important to include notes of the child's own view of their learning and the problem they think they may have. Questions to ask of assessment are:

- does this relate to real classroom activities?
- does this relate to long-term realistic goals?
- is what is being tested relevant to the learners themselves and will it enhance or damage their self-esteem?
- can this type of assessment be carried out within the time available and with the available resources of staff?
- are cross-curricular skills being assessed?
- can the pupil access the curriculum on offer?

Continuity between phases: Key Stage 2 to Key Stage 3

Transfer of information between phases, especially from primary to secondary schools, is a key issue for SEN. Schools should be clear about whose responsibility it is to:

- visit the previous school
- sift information given orally or on paper
- disseminate information in good time for distribution to all colleagues.

A key role for a secondary SENCO is to collate information from primary records. Many SENCOs spend much of their summer holiday doing paperwork to prepare records for the autumn term. Should this be their job or should year tutors share the task? There is still a tendency for teachers to say, 'Oh, I don't read records, they might prejudice me against a pupil.' *It cannot be stated too strongly that the correct flow of information between phases is essential for all pupils, but especially those with SEN.* If too much is in files, teachers in the next school cannot easily pick out priority areas of need. Records should indicate those most at risk, and secondary schools must make use of the information (see also Chapter 8).

Key Stage 3: a systems approach to identification

It is much more difficult to collate and collect new information about pupils with SEN in secondary schools. A pupil may only be causing concern in one or two subjects, or they may be finding difficulties across the curriculum and the whole school day. For a few pupils, transfer to secondary school is particularly traumatic and pupils need extra pastoral care. This means there must be a simple procedure to register new concerns and to send this information to a person with responsibility, usually the SENCO, but possibly the year head. Another system might be to have SEN representatives in each department who collate such individual records of concern. The advantage of this system is that it is more likely to result in a good differentiation and the use of appropriate resources in each department. A cross-over of such departmental information would be needed to ensure a 'whole-child approach'. This would almost certainly require the SENCO's help. Pastoral and health needs should be noted because these are likely to affect the pupil throughout the school day. Links between pastoral and curriculum systems must be planned to ensure information flows appropriately.

Pupils identified as having SEN require a summary document of their present functioning, standards of achievement, and priority needs, whether health, social or educational. Without betraying confidential material, it is essential that every subject teacher has a list of basic information about SEN pupils. This should include the potential effect on the learning processes for the child in question.

Schools are increasingly using computer-based systems for writing IEPs and for monitoring pupil progress. It is still important to make sure the pupils know and understand their own targets and feel they are making progress (see Source List 1).

Key Stage 4

For the majority of pupils identification of additional needs will have already been carried out at an earlier stage of their school life. For a few a notable change due to medical or other causes may need to be noted. Problems may arise at Key Stage 4 which make it necessary to seek exam concessions (see Chapter 5). If a student's work or behaviour deteriorates from previous standards, there will need to be discussion, observation and assessment to determine causes which could be medical or social in origin.

Now, with the alternative curriculum arrangements at Key Stage 4 allowing some degree of flexibility, pupils require opportunities to discuss alternative courses or arrangements (see Chapter 5).

Decisions and information flow concerning early identification

Decisions on the following points need writing into the school's policy in the identification section. Who needs to know about early identification?

- the SENCO: needs to know the name and basic information for those with additional needs;
- the class/subject teacher: in order to plan and differentiate teaching;
- the parents: so their views can be added to the information and their role in helping can be decided;
- the pupils: so their views are also recorded.

Who should do this? The identification and assessment is the class teacher's responsibility in primary schools. In secondary schools, the form tutor might be the best person to collate information, or possibly the year head. It cannot reasonably be left to the SENCO. Many needs are met by good curriculum planning and delivery, and in the monitoring of progress through good record-keeping. A small number of pupils, however, fail to make progress, despite their teacher's intervention. For these children who have extra requirements, planning is needed in order to 'fine tune' the programme of intervention more precisely. This requires a much more specialised form of planning known as an Individual Education Plan (IEP).

What is an Individual Education Plan?

The term 'Individual Education Plan' was originally used in the USA but in Britain it was only introduced universally with the Code of Practice (1994). Many LEAs had for many years developed sets of proformas to establish consistency across their schools in recording the staged assessment procedures first introduced in the Warnock report. These forms have been adapted to meet some of the additional requirements of the Code of Practice. In other LEAs, schools have evolved their own ways of recording an individual's progress. The essential features of an Individual Education Plan are listed in the Code of Practice (5:32).

The term IEP refers to both a process and a document. The document has two key purposes. The first is educational, for those identified as having additional needs. The second is accountability, providing evidence of what has been done for the individual child and recording parents', pupil's and teachers' professional views.

All early information that has been collected about concerns and all baseline assessments of the pupils will be used in the IEP. Information is also needed about the pupil's strengths and interests. This is important because it is through these strengths that positive progress will be made. The pupil's views must be sought as well as those of parents.

Writing and reviewing IEPs has caused some concern to schools and to their SENCOs. The purpose of an IEP is to collect information which indicates how best to teach the pupil and develop a plan of action, with targets which can be understood and achieved by the pupil and his or her teachers and parents. It must be accessible to everyone as a working document which will influence classroom practice. It has to be specific and achievable but must also be feasible to use in ordinary classrooms. Schools may be tempted to introduce the use of commercial packages to help with IEP writing, so-called Management Information Systems (MIS). These can prove helpful but as McKeown (2003) points out, staff training should be available, not just in the use of the software, but in realising that fine tuning to meet individual needs is still necessary. Data protection rules apply to these packages and parents must be told that electronic information is being stored. Both parent and child should have access to the record if they so wish.

An Individual Education Plan includes information about:
- the short-term targets set for or by the child
- the teaching strategies to be used
- the provision to be put in place
- when the plan is to be reviewed
- success and/or exit criteria
- outcomes (to be recorded when IEP is reviewed).

(Code of Practice 2001, 5:50)

Applied behavioural analysis, as in task analysis, has heavily influenced the planning of many IEPs. This often results in very small, behaviourally based targets, often related only to aspects of literacy or mathematics, being the most commonly used in IEPs. But targets have to be significant enough to affect the overall progress and well-being of the pupil who is working within the whole curriculum, and furthermore it must be possible for the class or subject teacher to build the targets into their lesson planning. The IEP document needs to reflect both the whole child and the whole curriculum. It also needs to identify priorities for the next period of time (usually a term). These priorities must matter to the pupil (see Appendix 3a for sample forms and guidelines on IEPs).

Checklist of key decisions about IEP writing:

- have the concerns about the pupil been expressed clearly, with enough information from all existing assessments to indicate present levels of achievement? (Baseline Assessment, NC and other assessment data)
- have the pupils' strengths and interests been recorded?
- have the pupil's views about their learning problems been noted?
- have parents' views and their potential roles for helping been included?
- have targets been set, with sufficient attention to relevance and reality for the pupil and teacher and criteria for success? These targets must be specific enough for it to be quite clear when they have been reached.
- have the necessary resources of time, support and equipment been noted?
- is the IEP document accessible to those who need it to work with the pupil?
- will it inform curriculum and lesson planning?
- have affective as well as cognitive needs been addressed?
- have any medical or pastoral needs been noted?
- has the **review** date been set?
- what part will the pupil and parents play in the review?
- when the review date comes, will there be evidence of the work done?
- how will the IEP information be summarised at the end of the school year or phase to pass on to the next class or school?
- how and by whom will the review process be monitored?

Review of Individual Education Plans

It is *essential* that pupils with IEPs have regular reviews. It may be much better if colleagues work together in year groups to review, one taking the questioning role and one the answering role. A planned timetable for IEP reviews is needed for every school. Time is such a scarce resource that it must be allocated formally for this process. It is a role for senior management to both allocate and safeguard this time for IEP reviews.

The SENCO will be involved in setting up the review process, acting as consultant to colleagues and helping in decision-making for those pupils for whom it is necessary to move to *School Action Plus*. Because of the labour-intensive nature of IEP reviews, the number of pupils in a school at this stage should be carefully considered. IEPs should enhance the school's policy and provision for those with SEN, not become a burden for all concerned. (See Source List 1 for further reading on IEPs.)

Decision about who requires School Action

Decisions on these questions need to be written into school policy under the section on identification procedures. Which pupils have significant needs that affect their progress in one or more aspects of the curriculum and will require a specialised and supported programme written on their IEP? The resource implications must be considered. Some of these needs might be best met through good use of group IEPs and support. Who needs to know about these pupils?

- the SENCO: to help advise on and resource the interventions;
- the class/subject teacher: to differentiate and plan effectively for pupils;
- the year head: for information;
- the parents: their views and their role to be recorded in supporting the child;
- the pupil: so they understand and agree to the targets set.

Who will ensure that time is available and the process is monitored carefully?

- the head: to make resource decisions and to inform governors.

Who will help? The SENCO will be called on for most of the help at this stage. However, support services, specifically educational psychologists and learning support teachers, can give advice at this stage in an informal way or through in-service training. Parents must also be involved at this decision point in the process.

School Action Plus

There will have been a working IEP for at least two terms and the pupil's learning styles and difficulties will be well known. However, pupils requiring more support will be causing additional concern because they are still not making expected progress. It is for this reason that outside agencies, in particular support services such as learning support teachers or educational psychologists, are called in to add their views. They add to the assessment information by carrying out a range of tests or observations or by working closely with the pupil.

Someone from a support service might therefore be invited to contribute to the information at a *School Action* review. It may be that, after the assessment from such a support service, the advice might be to maintain the pupil at *School Action*. If the advice is to move to *School Action Plus* then the purpose of the outsider's assessment is to advise on the IEP for the pupil. Further discussion of working with support services at *School Action Plus* follows in Chapter 7.

The number of pupils needing *School Action Plus* is often limited by the availability of local resources, which varies considerably across the country. After a period of assessment or support the pupil may well return to *School Action*. An IEP could, however, continue to be needed for such pupils throughout their whole school life. (Chapter 9 continues to discuss the coordination of *School Action Plus* and beyond.)

Referral for a statutory assessment

Very few pupils (1 to 2 per cent of the population) will have such severe and persistent difficulties that they cannot cope within mainstream education without significant additional provision. If the school has carried out all the work at school-based stages and after consultation with the support services and the parents they all agree to do so, a request is made by the head teacher to the LEA for a multi-disciplinary assessment. While this assessment is taking place the pupil will continue to have an IEP in place which is carefully monitored. Parents may also request such an assessment.

The SENCO will then be asked to collect and collate all documentation, IEPs and supporting evidence. Then, either they or the head will write to the LEA making a formal request for a statutory assessment. Most LEAs have proformas for such requests. If the LEA agrees to the assessment they have a duty under the Code to carry this out within six months. This may or may not result in a decision by the LEA to give a statement. If the LEA wishes, they can write a 'note in lieu' of a statement, which means the pupil's needs are discussed, but will be met at *School Action Plus*. Statements can be issued with or without resources. The draft statement is sent to the parents who can ask for changes to be made. If the LEA and the parents cannot agree to these changes or there is a dispute over placement decisions, the parent may take the matter to the SEN tribunal. But first, most LEAs will attempt to mediate a mutually satisfactory solution to the parents' request (see Chapter 9).

This chapter has been concerned with the majority of pupils who remain the responsibility of the school and whose needs are met through careful assessment and planning, reviewing and readjusting targets in response to progress. This assessment and recording process is *every* teacher's responsibility but the SENCO must keep comprehensive records and ensure the review process is carried out thoroughly. In order for this to be possible, the overall planning of time for reviews, the organisation of paperwork, and clear definition of roles and responsibilities needs to be part of the whole-school policy for SEN and to link to the school's assessment policy. Staff will benefit from training in writing IEPs and this again will nearly always be organised by the SENCO (see IEP guidelines, Appendix 3a). Such training needs should be identified as part of the SEN policy. The themes of this chapter are continued in Chapters 5 and 9.

CHAPTER 4

The Curriculum: Planning for an Inclusive Curriculum

The previous chapter concentrated on identifying and assessing pupils with SEN. The Code of Practice suggests this individual approach to the problems of SEN by its demands for detailed assessment and planning. This has had the effect of adding to the administrative and bureaucratic load on teachers and in particular on SENCOs. While no one would doubt that knowing more about individual children will help understand their needs, such information is only useful if action follows. The outcome of individual programming should help the pupil cope better with the demands of the curriculum and result in an increased rate of progress.

The problem for class and subject teachers is that children are not taught as individuals for much of their day, but in social groupings of up to 30. The teaching and learning process is therefore interactive. Within-child features play their part, but so do classroom organisation and resourcing, modes of curriculum delivery and teacher management style. Some educators, such as Bruner and Vygotsky, think that learning is best conceptualised as a social process, rather than an individual one.

Gipps (1992) explains that:

> The social constructivist model of learning assumes that knowledge is built up by the child in the form of connected schemata; the child is seen as an agent of his or her own learning activity constructing knowledge. (p. 3)

One of Vygotsky's key concepts was that of the 'zone of proximal development' (Vygotsky 1978). This describes the gap between what the child can do alone and what they can do with someone who has more knowledge or skill. Gipps further explains that:

> Vygotsky's model suggests that not all tasks should be perfectly matched to the child's current level of development, indeed some tasks should require a shift to the next 'zone of development'. But what is crucial to this idea, is that interaction with another person is essential, whether this person is a teacher or peer, to help move this moving-on process. (p. 4)

This suggests a key role for the teacher is to build a rich learning community in the classroom. The classroom is also part of the wider community of the school and the district. It must, however, be remembered that influences beyond the school, local and national, affect the focus of curriculum delivery and its assessment.

The National Curriculum

Since 1988 the National Curriculum in England and Wales has been the major outside influence on the curriculum in state schools. It offered every child the entitlement to a 'broad, balanced and differentiated' curriculum, across a range of *Programmes of Study* for the core and foundation subjects. It was recognised that this would require flexible planning by teachers.

> Within any group of pupils there will be a wide range of ability and experience. This calls for a flexible approach allowing differentiation to provide success and challenges for them all. (NCC 1989)

It has proved difficult to deliver all of these programmes to the full range of pupils, despite enormous efforts from teachers. The Dearing revision of the National Curriculum in 1994 gave more flexibility. The School Curriculum and Assessment Authority Access Statement stated that the flexibility of the new orders allowed material to be selected, where necessary, from an earlier Key Stage Programme of Study to enable individual pupils, with or without statements for SEN, to progress and demonstrate achievement. This material was to be presented within the context suitable for the pupil's age (SCAA 1996).

The Code of Practice (2001), referring to the National Curriculum Inclusion Statement, suggests ways in which the curriculum can be effective in offering learning opportunities for all pupils. There are three principles which should be considered when developing a more inclusive curriculum:

(a) setting suitable learning challenges;
(b) responding to pupils' diverse learning needs;
(c) overcoming potential barriers to learning and assessment for individuals and groups of pupils.

This could result in fewer IEPs being written for individual children. Much can be done by modifications to schemes of work and through short- and long-term planning. Even when the overall content does not change, different amounts of time might be allocated to particular skills or experiences in any one time period. Time management of the curriculum becomes very important when tailoring to the needs of a particular population of a school or classroom. When planning lessons or short-term schemes of work, it will be important to consider what barriers to learning each lesson may produce for the range of pupils in a particular class, which might include children with disabilities as well as a range of learning styles. As far as possible, flexible delivery of the content and creative thinking about assessment modalities can reduce the learning difficulties of many students.

The IEP within differentiation

Where pupils do require an IEP, SENCOs should not be left to deal with the planning in isolation because, if they are, their colleagues delivering the curriculum will be less effective in ensuring progress. For the IEP to be useful to teachers and pupils, some questions will need answering:

- How will priorities and targets be jointly agreed between teacher, pupil and parent, so that all can understand what is expected?
- Should the IEP cover the whole curriculum? (Could a cross-curricular target be chosen, e.g. presentation of work, use of IT as access?) How will this information be communicated to all relevant staff? Should there be a target for literacy, numeracy and behaviour as the Code suggests?
- Should the IEP focus on one or two small steps, related to mastery of basic skills? This may produce the best success rate and show evidence of progress, but how frequently will such targets need reviewing?
- How will the IEP affect the curriculum planning for the teacher? Will the class or subject teachers have read the IEP and use the targets of individual pupils as objectives for groups within the class?

But the most important question when writing IEPs may be: How will all of this affect classroom teaching and organisation?

The activity on staff development (see Activity 3) provides a useful way to find answers to these questions (see Figure 4.1).

Teachers must first be very clear about the following:
- What are the core curriculum objectives for this lesson or series of lessons? How do these relate to National Curriculum programmes of study?
  (These may have been selected by the year group to fit into joint topics.)
- How will these core objectives be assessed, i.e. how will teachers know if the pupils have reached a satisfactory level of skills and understanding of key concepts? Does the assessment also need to be differentiated? Will this be recorded as part of the IEP?

Additional planning for individuals

- Have the pupils (the whole class) the prerequisite skills and knowledge of concepts to begin to reach these objectives? What are the prerequisite skills for this core objective? These need to be clearly defined.
- Have the pupils with SEN these prerequisite skills and concepts? (Cross reference to IEPs will be most useful here.)
- What modification will be necessary for pupils who have not mastered these prerequisite skills or concepts? Will they need 'pre-teaching' or a different resource to assist access to information, or a different core objective?

Further questions related to continuity and whole-school issues

- Additional questions can then be asked about whole-school or department planning. Using this approach also helps develop cross-curricular skills and concepts. What will the pupils bring from another curriculum area that can be of use within this lesson?
- How can a resource bank be built up which can be shared to assist in differentiation of topics? Much published material is now available, but artefacts and games etc. may need to be added.
- How does all of this affect continuity issues and grouping arrangements in school?

Figure 4.1 Lesson planning for differentiation

Some alternative ways of thinking about pedagogy

The second half of this chapter looks at ways of conceptualising pupils' learning within a differentiated curriculum. Approaches are discussed which may help focus on learning styles or experiences, rather than attainment levels, within a set content-based curriculum. The approaches discussed cover three ways of thinking about learning: (a) behavioural, (b) cognitive, in particular thinking skills programmes, and (c) affective, considering the emotional needs of the learner.

The influence of behavioural science on SEN curriculum and pedagogy

In the last two decades special needs curriculum planning and pedagogy have been strongly influenced by behavioural theories. Based largely on applied behavioural analysis these are a development of Skinner's operant conditioning theory of learning. Skinner believed that by manipulating the environment, you could change an organism's behaviour (Skinner 1974). First you began by deciding on the goal to be reached and then you shaped the behaviour by a system of reinforcement of successive approximations towards that goal. The reinforcement was food (in work with pigeons) but could be praise when working with people! Skinner argued strongly that his 'science of behaviour' could include a world view of how the environment influenced man's behaviour and indeed his culture.

During the 1980s, educational psychologists, in particular, promoted an applied behavioural approach to the analysis of learning difficulties and their remediation. As Norwich (1990a) suggests, this may have been due to a growing dissatisfaction and lack of confidence in the validity of psychometric testing and its relationship to intervention. He further explains that:

> A behaviourist approach discounts what is not directly observable. What the child can do now is what is assessed. It also is concerned with intended outcomes of the learner rather than what the teacher intends to do or present to the learner. (p. 90)

The point here is that the outcomes are chosen and predetermined by the teacher and the child 'shaped' towards these outcomes by the process of rewarding successive steps. This is the task analysis approach that has become firmly embedded in SEN teaching and is visible in the IEP approach of the Code of Practice.

Behavioural objectives are small-scale and can only be concerned with observable behaviours. Curriculum objectives are on a larger scale and are not confined to what is observable, although outcomes have to be measured in some way through assessment. Task analysis concerns itself with a learner's individual steps towards the chosen goal; it has less to say about teaching methods to obtain those goals, and nothing to say about any inner processes which may apply. The principle of the task analysis approach is that success in the small steps will make a successful learner, who can then tackle new steps. There is evidence that this does work within the confines of the chosen focus. Learning, acquired through a small-step programme, must then be generalised and synthesised into the context of the curriculum. This last step is often neglected.

Wedell's (1980) model of compensatory interaction was to influence thinking about individual needs, post 1981. There was a move away from seeing learning difficulties as all 'within-child'. The curriculum in school and the influences from home were seen to have a part to play. The responsibility for both *causing* as well as *curing* SEN fell on teachers who were then encouraged to look at their strategies and pedagogy. It was stated that overuse of objectives could lead to:

- narrowing of the curriculum
- segregation of pupils
- teachers feeling inadequate
- pupils being passive
- the curriculum becoming static.

(Ainscow and Tweddle 1988, p. 29)

Wedell also encouraged teachers to negotiate with the learner about objectives and to observe the pupils' preferred learning styles. The fear of a mechanistic and technical approach to education remains, and a further problem is the sheer impossibility of working at the individual small step scale when coping with large classes and with very little help.

So how can the experience of using the behavioural approach continue to be useful to those planning the differentiated curriculum for SEN?

- Objectives thinking has led to a clearer conceptualisation of individual priorities and clearer definition of needs.
- Baseline assessment has been a useful starting point on which to build programmes.
- Goal and target-setting, if carried out in partnership with the pupil and teacher, can increase self-worth and the child's responsibility for monitoring achievement. Evidence can be collected through observation to prove achievement.
- Planning small steps to achieve success has proved worthwhile with the developmentally young or where the task is skill based.

● Individual priorities and goals can feed forward to inform both curriculum planning and differentiation and help teachers think about appropriate strategies to help pupils meet their targets.

This behavioural model of learning has strongly influenced the way teachers have planned target-setting for IEPs, despite its shortcomings. One shortcoming is that, by concentrating only on what can be observed, little account is taken of inner processes of thinking and feeling. Not only does this feel sterile, it discounts huge areas of human activity and culture. The behavioural model is also very 'teacher led', giving only limited autonomy to the pupil. There is therefore an argument for considering alternative approaches to teaching and learning, for example a model which enhances the cognitive thinking process, through planned teacher mediation.

Cognitive development and thinking skills programmes

Piaget's theories of cognitive development state that a child goes through stages: first, concrete operational, and then in adolescence, formal operational thinking (Inhelder and Piaget 1958). The debate about Piaget's stages and ages lies outside the scope of the present discussion. Suffice to say that Piaget and others who extended ideas on cognitive development (Bruner 1968, Donaldson 1978) had significant effects on the pedagogy of the primary 'process' curriculum. However, it is the move into formal operational thinking which is most important in secondary education and which may cause problems for those with learning difficulties.

Cognitive interventions based on formal operational thinking

Formal operational thinking emerges during the secondary school years. It is mediated through environmental and social interaction, but is not tied to any particular subject area. The most significant attempt to intervene and change the learning potential of young people of this age group was that of Reuven Feuerstein in the 1950s. Building on a mixture of psychometrics and theories of Piaget and Vygotsky, Feuerstein evolved a solution to the sociological problem of the new immigrants arriving in Israel. These young people were not able to take places in the traditional education system and were initially labelled as backward.

Feuerstein, a clinical psychologist, challenged both the traditional trust in IQ tests and the view that intelligence was a once and for all endowment. Feuerstein *et al.* (1980) said that the thinking skills we need in order to learn effectively, which are normally absorbed by children as they develop in their family and culture, can, if absent, be instrumentally remedied. Feuerstein developed a theory of mediated learning experiences and a programme of structured exercises known as instrumental enrichment (IE). Based on an analysis of the cognitive functions required by learners, the IE course consists of 13 instruments, containing between one and two dozen activities and intended to be taught at a frequency of five hours a week, for at least two years. Feuerstein wished this to be free of all traditional school subject matter. (See Feuerstein *et al.* 1980, and Appendix 4a for further information.)

His work opened up a whole new field of cognitive education which spread beyond Israel to the USA, Canada, South America, Russia and some countries in Europe. In the early 1980s officers from several LEAs in England visited the United States and on return agreed to train teachers and set up IE projects. Their work was evaluated by a Schools Council publication (Weller and Craft 1983). One project published the materials known as Somerset Thinking Skills (Blagg *et al.* 1988). These materials help pupils to synthesise information, analyse data, and appreciate their own strategies of thinking.

In England, cognitive intervention programmes could not remain free of subject content. Possibly this was due to pressure of time, certainly once the National Curriculum began. Those who developed programmes may also have felt that these would have more validity to teachers, pupils and the public if the results could be measured in improvements in increased attainments in subject assessments. The best researched and most successful was CASE (Cognitive Acceleration through Science), a project led by Shayer and colleagues between 1984 and 1987.

> CASE materials were designed to address individually the schemata of formal operations and incorporate the principles . . . into a set of activities whose content was overtly scientific. (Adey and Shayer 1994)

This project had measurable success which lasted over time, the effects of which could be seen two years later in GCSE results. In their evaluation of their project the authors emphasise the need for this type of intervention to have 'duration and density' if it is to be effective. By duration they mean that it should take place over at least a two-year period. They further comment that it is not packaged materials and activities which give a new method its power, however useful as a framework. It depends on thorough staff development, which includes knowledge of the theory of the method, demonstration of skills, followed by practice, feedback and coaching on classroom presentation. Only then will mediated learning take place which really raises standards. However, as Norwich (1990b) says:

> The point is not to advocate Instrumental Enrichment as such, but to illustrate the point that cross-curricula skills may need additional emphasis for some children with SEN. (p. 25)

The cognitive demand of materials and methods

Materials used by teachers – textbooks, worksheets and other written materials – make two types of demand of readers. One is cognitive, the other based on reading skills. Readability is often assessed by word length and the number of syllables, but is more usefully addressed by looking at features such as legibility, complexity of syntax, amount of specialist vocabulary and interest level. The cognitive demand of materials can be assessed using a taxonomy of knowledge.

Using Bloom's Taxonomy to evaluate learning resources

Bloom's taxonomies of cognitive and affective domains of knowledge could provide such a framework for curriculum planning and a checklist against which curriculum content can be judged for its value, balance and intellectual demand. The aim is to develop higher order thinking skills by offering able pupils, in particular, sufficient challenge. The first two levels of the taxonomy are knowledge and comprehension. Few materials or methods move beyond this to application, analysis, synthesis or evaluation – the other levels of the taxonomy. (See Appendix 4b for further information.)

Lessons to be learnt from cognitive interventions

What then are the lessons that can be learnt from cognitive interventions and cognitive analysis of pedagogy? The answers may be that:

- Underachievement may be due to a lack of suitable strategies for thinking.
- Pupils *can* be taught thinking skills if the *how* of learning is addressed as well as the *what*.
- Thinking skills can be taught through curriculum subjects, where the use of analogy can help concept development.

- When pupils are taught thinking processes, they gain control of their own learning and this increases motivation and self-esteem.

To do all of the above, teachers will need to learn how to:

- Identify the stage of cognitive development reached by a pupil or group.
- Examine the demand of the curriculum content and materials on offer and adapt these or prepare pupils to meet the demands.
- Analyse faulty processes of thinking at the input, elaboration and output phases of lessons and understand the component parts of these processes (see Appendix 4a).
- Mediate learning through group discussions and by direct teaching of strategies to improve thinking processes.
- Teach pupils to reflect on and vocalise their own thinking processes.

Affective perspectives

Emotional states are an important part of the curriculum for many reasons. Wragg (1997) argues that emotional development could be considered as a subject on the curriculum or a cross-curricular issue and that it certainly is something that pupils and teachers must understand. 'In positive form emotions offer a stimulation and enhancement to pupils' learning, in negative form they can be a killer of it.' (p. 81).

It is important to recognise that many aspects of the curriculum can feed children's emotional growth. Children need help to explore their own feelings and those of others. One way to keep this on the agenda is by becoming more aware of those aspects of the curriculum which help the understanding of the emotions of others, explore the nature of relationships and make sense of how other people overcome obstacles. Opportunities can be given to explore affective responses to particular themes. This will happen when there is

> A climate of warmth and support in which self confidence and self esteem can grow and in which pupils feel valued and able to risk making mistakes as they learn without fear of failure. (NCC 1989)

The world of story, poetry, dance and drama, art and music has a therapeutic role to play, as well as being part of the cultural entitlement for all pupils. Sometimes artistic subjects are seen as having lower prestige than subjects which represent instrumental spheres of knowledge, like science, but it is important that areas of understanding which have a personal characteristic are valued to the same degree. It is often through the creative activities that pupils who were otherwise unremarkable begin to shine and achieve. Once this happens, the growth in self-confidence can be harnessed for their less favourite subjects. The other virtue of creative subjects or teaching methods is that they allow open-ended outcomes which are not predetermined and pupils' individual achievements can be accepted. Differentiation by outcome is the norm. These aspects of the curriculum can feed the child, enrich language and ideas, and encourage creative and problem-solving responses. They come nearer to the early years experiences of play, especially when taught by enthusiastic teachers.

Hanko (1995) argues that the curriculum can help pupils to understand the human condition and the part emotions play in people's lives. She comments that teachers do not always realise the full potential of the opportunities the curriculum offers to explore feelings and help pupils build their self-worth. She suggests this may in part be because 'teachers have been side tracked into mistaking surface behaviour management as a sufficient response to behaviour problems' (p. 76). She adds that:

> Accounts of experiences of concern to pupils can be introduced and through discussion children can speak of their own experiences but also explore in general terms what is

reflected in the literature provided. Through use of consultancy groups teachers can find ways of linking personal experience to curriculum content.

(See also Chapter 6 on support groups.)

All of the above takes place within the social context of the classroom. Managing this environment so that it produces a positive influence on pupils' thinking, feeling and learning is *the* key skill of the teachers. The environment must be flexible enough to foster learning and support autonomy, and structured enough to give security to pupils and to set boundaries. Effective classrooms set within effective schools will support all pupils, but especially those with SEN. Fundamental to all of this is a whole-school culture and ethos which values individuals and allows everyone, teachers and pupils alike, to contribute to the learning process.

Developing inclusive curriculum delivery

Positive learning environments

For any curriculum to be delivered effectively, a positive learning environment is essential. This in turn requires pupils to fit in with normal classroom routines and rules and to respect the rights of others. Certain pupils with learning or emotional and behavioural difficulties (EBD) present a challenge to teachers. It is outside the scope of this section to explore class management or EBD in depth. The important point to remember is that curriculum aims include the promotion of spiritual, moral and cultural development of all children. It follows that helping children learn how to work in a harmonious way, so that everyone is respected and valued, is part of the entitlement curriculum.

For the SENCO to be effective in educational, rather than administrative terms, is therefore a challenge. But it could be argued that it is only when those with detailed knowledge of individual differences and learning styles meet with those who plan and deliver lessons, that changes to teaching and learning will occur.

The information from good IEPs should feed forward to schemes of work and lesson planning, so that there is greater flexibility in delivering the curriculum to meet the diversity of the full range of pupils in classrooms.

Develop a learning institution which is responsive to feedback

This means making full use of records and assessment information, including IEPs, to plan schemes of work and lessons. In many cases this will require detailed knowledge of individual pupils and their progress, which may come best from learning support staff and their observations. At a strategic level this requires liaison time to be built into the timetable so that effective planning can take place concerning delivery of the curriculum. The DRC Code (2002) makes it clear that schools have a duty to ensure equality of access to the curriculum, as this is a right of all pupils.

Involve the parents and pupils in the curricular planning process

Parents are very aware that schools should remember individual needs when planning curriculum delivery. Parents of pupils with complex needs often have different priorities for their child. These concern personal, social and life skills. Parents can also problem-solve and have particular roles to play as they see their child from a different perspective from that of the teachers. Parents can remind teachers to think in a cross-curricular way so that the child is not totally overwhelmed or confused by different approaches to topics. Some pupils react adversely to change and need preparation which parents can provide if they are involved early enough. Parents know, for example, how long ordinary tasks like eating and dressing can take for some children with complex disabilities. Parents can remind staff that homework also takes longer than average. All of these types of information can be used when planning IEPs, but may also have more general implications for school policies.

Develop a team approach to curricular planning

Support is often the method of differentiation most often chosen for special educational needs work. Support can be conceptualised as support for the pupil, but also as curriculum support with the class teacher. Best practice is when support personnel and teachers work as a team. The team can be extended to include visiting specialists, such as peripatetic teachers and therapists for those with more complex needs. The role of this team is to be as creative as possible in integrating the special requirements of the individual into normal class delivery of the curriculum. Other pupils often enjoy doing activities or games which may originally have been designed for an individual.

Review resources regularly

Some pupils will have additional resources to help them access the curriculum. Some of these are technical in nature. Equipment must be kept in good condition, with spare parts and switches available. Pupils may need training to use this equipment efficiently, for example keyboard skills may need to be taught by a suitable instructor. The learning community of the classroom will support a wealth of diversity itself, if flexibly managed and democratically controlled. When pupils have joint purposes with teachers they can carry forward individuals whose needs may be quite great and who on their own would struggle to make any progress.

Concluding thoughts

These four sections have been included to give food for thought when planning intervention programmes or thinking of different ways of delivering the curriculum to motivate learning. Clearly most curriculum planning and development of pedagogy and resources are issues for whole-school development. SENCOs can use their particular skills and knowledge, and their depth and breadth of understanding of curriculum issues to:

- Draw attention to pupils' individual differences and abilities, including their *strengths*, which build on the pupils' *strengths and real-world experiences*.
- Remind colleagues that, for many pupils, the role of the teacher is to *mediate* learning so that the pupil makes connections between their previous experience and the new material.
- Help the school to work pro-actively to meet SEN by being a *change agent* for curriculum planning.
- Inform senior management and governors of the priority areas for SEN curriculum developments. This will help governors to decide how to share resources *between and amongst* pupils with SEN, as required by the SEN policy demands of Circular 6/94, Regulation 1.

The next chapter gives some further practical guidance about the SENCO's role in relation to differentiating each of the Key Stages of the National Curriculum.

CHAPTER 5

The Curriculum: Key Issues for Key Stages

This chapter looks at some of the characteristic features of the curriculum within each phase of education. Suggestions are made about the SENCO's role in helping colleagues plan and deliver a differentiated Programme of Study facilitating inclusive education for all pupils, including those with SEN.

Early years (3–5 year olds)

The main characteristic of the early years curriculum is that it is firmly based on the knowledge of children's development. Play is given a prominent place, but play which is structured to encourage intellectual, social, aesthetic and physical development. The environment of the classroom should be stimulating – encouraging exploration, questioning, experimentation and problem-solving. The adults, led by the teacher, set up and mediate the learning experiences of the child, often by engaging in conversation which promotes the child's use of language. Stories and rhymes extend the child's repertoire of language experience into the world of symbolic representation.

Because meeting the individual differences in development is part of an early years teacher's skills, almost every child with SEN can be included. When joining the reception class, children should have a wide vocabulary, be keen to learn and to take on the challenge of beginning reading and number work. Research (Tizard and Hughes 1984) shows that early experiences at home and nursery affect the skills which children have on entering school. Impoverished experience predisposes children to have more difficulties with school subjects.

There are two main groups of SEN typically found in nursery and reception classes. The first group includes children whose needs were identified pre-school, by parents and health professionals. They may have physical or sensory impairment or be significantly delayed in all round development. Others may have difficulties with language and communication. Many of this group will have statements or programmes already devised by advisory teachers, or others such as Portage workers (a home-based early intervention programme aimed at teaching parents how to teach pre-school children).

The second group are those whose needs emerge during the early years of schooling. Typical of this group are children with speech and language difficulties, or those whose social skills are poorly developed and who find conforming to group situations very difficult. For behaviour problems, support from educational psychologists may be appropriate. Speech and language therapists are in short supply and usually see children outside school at clinics, although collaborative schemes are being developed in some areas. Help from visiting advisory teachers for SEN may be most useful in planning curriculum interventions to enhance language development.

The Code of Practice (2001) offers advice on early years settings in Chapter 4. The Early Years Development and Childcare Partnerships (EYDCP) bring together a diverse range of early years provision which becomes eligible for government funding. All of these settings are required to have regard to the Code of Practice (2001) and the DRC Code of Practice (2002). There is also a requirement to have a written SEN policy. Early education provision is part of the foundation stage of education for children aged 3–5 years.

Foundation Curriculum Guidance (QCA 2000) provides advice on six areas of learning:

● personal, social and emotional development
● communication, language and literacy
● mathematical development
● knowledge and understanding of the world
● physical development
● creative development

The Early Learning goals set out what most children will have achieved by the end of the reception year. In the section on special educational needs and disabilities the QCA states that 'the focus should be on removing barriers for children where these already exist and in preventing learning difficulties from developing' (p. 14).

It must be remembered that the style of learning at this age should take into account the needs of the developing child. Development may be slower in some areas. *This does not in itself constitute a special educational need.*

The role of the early years SENCOs

● Working with parents to establish firm partnerships as early as possible, ensuring liaison between parents and a variety of agencies who offer advice and devise specialist programmes.
● Advising and supporting early years practitioners. This includes the early identification of pupils whose needs emerge in these years.
● Ensuring that appropriate IEPs are in place for those thus identified.
● Training LSAs and others who work with teachers to support children with SEN.

Key Stage 1, Years 5–7

Much of what is true of early years education continues to be true for Key Stage 1. There is the added pressure to meet the demands of the National Curriculum, in particular of teaching literacy and numeracy. A priority will be identifying literacy difficulties early and building in extra support through use of peer and parent partnership programmes.

The literacy and numeracy hours

The aim of the National Literacy and Numeracy Strategies is to give all children more opportunities to increase their skills in reading, spelling, writing and numeracy. However, care must still be taken of those who cannot keep up with the pace of the class and need more structured reading programmes built around their identified needs. These children also need rich experiences of literature and opportunities to talk about stories and pictures, as well as learning how to decode and encode print (Reason and Boote 1994).

The highly structured nature of the literacy and numeracy hours may benefit many children with special needs, if planned to include a range of abilities. Teaching Assistants (TAs) are increasingly being employed to help with groups in the literacy hour, but it is important that they have sufficient training and support from the class teacher for this task.

SENCOs need to balance the desire to include everyone in these hours with the individual needs of children who may not cope with or not be ready for some elements of this type of whole-class teaching. Neither the National Literacy nor the Numeracy Strategy should be seen as a rigid framework. As Briggs (2000) says, 'equality of opportunity does not always mean the same in terms of attainment or the speed and style of learning'. (For further help see Source List 1, Literacy and numeracy.)

Evaluation of the Literacy Hour

As Wall (2003) points out, 'The Literacy Hour has increased the amount of whole-class teaching, resulting in teachers struggling to include pupils with a wide range of disabilities and achieve demanding objectives.' If the strategy is adhered to it is unlikely to meet the learning needs of normal primary classes let alone those with additional needs. It would seem that the way forward is to use the framework, provided that there is flexibility to match the context and population of the particular school. Wall (2003) continues by saying 'teachers must be encouraged to continue to use their professional judgments about what is the most appropriate pedagogy for the children they teach' (p. 40).

A broad balanced curriculum

Remember that children continue to need a stimulating, enriching experience that challenges them to ask questions, explore and think. Concepts are developed through structured play, drama and creative activities, as well as through exposure to stories and poetry. It will be important to find which areas of the curriculum enhance the pupil's self-esteem and give opportunities to show their strengths. Classroom organisation and effective use of groups and of any adult help available, are the keys to meeting individual and special needs in this age group.

For all pupils it is important to remember the link between learning and emotional needs. Friendships are very important to pupils at this age. Personal and social education has a critical part to play in helping children become aware of others' perspectives. A popular development is the use of 'circle time', which aims to help children develop self-esteem, social skills, and the ability to see others' perspectives (see Source List 1, Individual Education Plans).

Key issues for SENCOs and class teachers

- Ensure careful recording of literacy and numeracy progress, noting children's preferred strategies and learning modalities. (Record these on the IEP.)
- Remember that some children need language enrichment, and opportunities to talk or listen to stories and share books with an adult in small groups.
- Provide sufficient and varied resources to meet individual needs: a range of suitable books, tapes, computer software, concept keyboards, etc.
- Address classroom management issues and the structure of curriculum delivery, to maximise teacher and adult interaction with pupils and to encourage pupil independence.
- Support positive relationships, which enhance self-esteem of pupils by giving value to individual achievement, and encouraging listening activities like 'circle time'.
- Remind teachers that children develop at different rates. Also remember that summer-born children are often at an earlier stage of development and will continue to need the activities of the early years stage to be available. *They may have developmental, not special, needs.*

● Work closely with parents, to keep them informed but also to involve them as much as possible in the work on their children's targets.
(For further information about resources and for further reading that relates to the above, see Source Lists.)

Key Stage 2, junior Years 7–11

The demands of the curriculum increase during these years, making a child-centred approach more difficult. The characteristic of these junior years is that pupils with moderate or specific learning difficulties become more visible, along with those whose emotional and behavioural difficulties block their progress. Together, these groups often make up the majority identified as having SEN. The challenge for teachers is to cover the individual needs of basic skills in reading, spelling, handwriting and mathematics, while at the same time giving full access to a broad, balanced curriculum. In both the literacy and numeracy hours care will need to be taken to plan group work to meet individual learning difficulties or cover lost ground.

It is in the area of classroom management strategies and relationships that teachers require most help. A tension is created by the need to meet individual needs as demanded by the IEP, while increasing the overall standards in literacy and numeracy. Effective use of group work, particularly when other adults are available for support, seems one solution; increasing pupils' independence through self-organised learning, is another.

Developing thinking and social skills

There are a number of published schemes to help children develop their problem-solving and thinking skills. Some, such as Lipman et al.'s (1980) *Philosophy in the Classroom*, encourage children to discuss ideas from stories which have been read aloud. The teacher helps children to listen to each other, take turns in speaking and conducts the dialogue so that children learn to follow a line of argument and express their own ideas. When used in this way these programmes appear to improve speaking and listening, higher order reading skills, and moral awareness. The most useful feature of all these programmes seems to be the awareness gained of *metacognition*, that is the ability to reflect on one's own thinking processes.

Disaffected pupils

Circular 10/99 outlines legal procedures and good practice for managing pupils with very difficult behaviour, especially those at risk of exclusion. For pupils who do not respond to the school's actions and may need longer term interventions, a Pastoral Support Programme (PSP) should be set up with external services. The advice is that PSPs should not be used for pupils with IEPs or statements of SEN. This circular points out that difficult behaviour may be the result of unmet special needs, thus early identification and suitable support are a priority for such pupils. The circular also points out that children in care may be particularly vulnerable. It is suggested that it is good practice that a named teacher should take responsibility for the coordination with carers and Social Services. IEPs should therefore be planned to take into account both the learning and social needs of these pupils.

SENCOs and teachers can work together to:

● Find ways of improving classroom management and organisation, including effective use of support staff and productive group work. Offer each other support, particularly with challenging pupil behaviour.

- Maximise peer group support through well resourced group activities: teaching pupils strategies of working collaboratively and solving problems together.
- Maximise use of any available adult help to reduce group size for key activities requiring mediated learning or specific teaching of skills.
- Aim to improve pupils' self-esteem and motivation to learn, increasing their autonomy and celebrating success.
- Improve lesson planning, using IEP information and specialist skills to contribute to curriculum differentiation including the literacy and numeracy hours.
- Teach thinking and study skills and apply these to the handling of information needed for other subject areas.
- Encourage use of appropriate information technology: taped books, computer programmes and alternative ways of recording work.
- Continue to work closely with parents and carers, involving them in target-setting and giving them a role in helping their child.

Assessment arrangement: Key Stages 2 and 3

SENCOs need to be up to date with current special assessment arrangements for the end of Key Stages 2 and 3, which may change each year. Details are available from the Qualifications and Curriculum Authority. Permission for special arrangements is required by specified dates.

Key Stage 3, 11–14 years

Many of the characteristics of Key Stage 2 continue to apply. New features are the scale of the organisation in secondary schools and the need to work with all curriculum areas and the pastoral system. *Communication is therefore the key issue.* This begins by communication between phases and dissemination of important information to all staff about the pupils that they will teach. Staff should be given key information in time to plan before mistakes are made at the critical transfer period (see Chapter 8). For the pupil, it is important that as curriculum pressure increases, a sense of achievement can still be maintained. This means setting up systems so that the dissemination of relevant information about students' needs is given to all staff and influences their curriculum delivery. The majority of targets set with the pupil should be challenging but achievable within normal differentiated curriculum delivery and class management.

The SENCO, or learning support team, should ideally be available to give advice and help staff development across departments on strategies for class management, differentiation by task, resources and support. Another key role will be the organisation of support for pupils with statements, as well as those on the school-based stages of the Code of Practice. The support team also can encourage styles of teaching which take into account a variety of learning styles and help pupils develop successful learning strategies. Partnership teaching may be an effective way to share expertise between the learning support staff and others. These options are not possible if all the support comes from teaching assistants.

Attention should also be paid to the effects on pupils' motivation of particular organisational features, such as banding and streaming. In some schools pupils are withdrawn for extra help in literacy and while this may be valuable it is important to keep in mind the rights of all pupils to take full part in the life of the school.

Structures for meetings, within and between departments, will need to be worked out as part of whole-school policy. Subject departments could, for example, have a link teacher for SEN, who meets with the SENCO on a regular basis. Links to the pastoral system are vital, so that learning support teachers, form tutors and heads of year communicate important information about students' needs and actions taken. Examples of good practice can be found in the companion book to this one, Cowne (2003) *Developing Inclusive Practice.* Target-setting for all pupils can be linked to systems of academic tutoring aimed at raising achievement for all.

Key issues for the Learning Support Department are:

- Collecting information from each department about an individual pupil's progress and sharing relevant information with colleagues.
- Designing IEPs with pupils, so that targets are challenging and achievable and self-esteem enhanced. Reviewing these frequently.
- Dissemination of SEN information amongst relevant staff and departments, including special assessment arrangements at end of Key Stage 3.
- Supporting curriculum development and differentiation, practically, with ideas on teaching and learning styles.
- Encouraging the teaching of study skills and checking on readability of texts and worksheets.
- Informing senior management of time and resources needed between and among pupils with SEN (a key issue in the SEN policy).
- Monitoring the effects of organisational features, such as setting, on pupil motivation and disaffection.
- Continuing to work closely with parents, keeping them informed and listening to problems. Some of these arise round homework. This can be difficult for SEN pupils. The SENCO may need to mediate between subject teacher and pupil to make homework demands reasonable for the family and pupil.
- Ensuring that students have access to careers guidance, working in partnership with career staff or services at the end of Key Stage 3.
- Being aware of those students who will need special exam arrangements so that this can be built into support work at Key Stage 4.

Key Stage 4

At Key Stage 4 the issue about differentiation or modification changes to one about choice of courses and subjects. SENCOs have an important role to play within the school's decision-making about what courses should be on offer. With their knowledge of student perspectives gained through negotiation of IEPs at Key Stage 3, and by working with careers consultants and parents, they will know much about the aspirations and capabilities of SEN students. This knowledge can influence the school's policy and planning in how option choices are put together.

Schools should look at the [*Section 400 List published annually by the DfEE*]. This will tell them which accredited qualifications have been approved for pupils of compulsory school age. SENCOs need to make themselves aware of what has been approved for use. Schools will be encouraged to consider more flexibility for some of their older pupils who might be more motivated by vocational courses, including work placements. Up to 15 per cent of the existing curriculum time could be available for those pupils who meet the criteria for such courses.

Much of this requires whole-school planning and is, as QCA suggests, for school staff, governors and parents to discuss in order to determine the purposes, principles and possibilities surrounding Key Stage 4 choices. The SENCO has a vital role in bringing the SEN perspective to these important discussions. A full discussion of all that is on offer at Key Stage 4 lies outside the scope of this book. QCA regularly publishes documents on Key Stage 4 and SENCOs need to keep up to date with the current situation, which is changing rapidly at present.

The revised curriculum also gives particular flexibility at Key Stage 4 to attend school part-time. It is now possible for disaffected youngsters in KS4 to be placed in an alternative programme which aims to give them skills related to work and the adult world and to build their confidence and self-esteem. But it is very important for students with special needs to leave school with qualifications and certificates that will help them get work. This means that the opportunities at KS4 must be relevant to the pupils, but also valued by others such as parents, further education providers and employers.

Now that there is a reduction in the number of subjects which must be taken, schools may disapply two subjects from design and technology, modern foreign languages and science. The revised National Curriculum now requires schools to teach citizenship. The personal and social health education programme (PHSE) will also help schools to develop cross-curricular skills and vocational courses.

Circular 10/99 requires a Pastoral Support Programme (PSP) to be put in place for disaffected pupils at risk of exclusion. Liaison with Learning Support is essential, as is partnership with parents or carers. Certain students may move to Pupil Referral Units as part of this programme, others may have a planned move to another school, or to a further education college in some cases. In all cases liaison between pastoral teams and the learning support department is essential.

Special exam arrangements at KS4

Schools must present information about students requiring special arrangements on the relevant form for each examination board or type of externally assessed qualification. Most accrediting boards ask for an educational psychologist's or specialist teacher's report. Each course has guidance notes so it will be necessary to be familiar with those boards chosen by the school. This may well be a cross-curricular issue and will require coordination. Subject staff will need to know about the types of arrangement possible and about student needs. Special arrangements might include use of a reader or a computer. The student must be used to the processes chosen. This means plans for special arrangements must be in place well before the exam period. It is likely that the SENCO will have an important role in the coordination of paperwork for the students in question.

Further education

Colleges of FE do not usually have a post equivalent to that of a SENCO. There are however an increased number of personnel appointed to learning support roles. The management of these staff and issues relating to SEN organisation and management are gradually being addressed by colleges. At the FE stage it is essential to pay attention to the young person's viewpoints, remembering that many students find it difficult to receive support which may draw unwanted attention to their disability.

Key roles and issues for the learning support department at KS4

- Early counselling and target-setting in partnership with both students and parents about programmes of study choices. This should be based on a range of evidence including baseline scores, SATs and teacher observations and finding ways to demonstrate pupils' strengths by choosing suitable accredited courses and using other records of achievement.
- Considered and mutual decisions about appropriate modification of some Programmes of Study as is possible in design and technology, modern foreign languages and science, so as to allow students greater opportunities for concentration and reinforcement in chosen areas.
- Helping students to self-regulate and monitor their own progress and helping colleagues to recognise the students' strengths and not to emphasise weaknesses.
- Provision of assessment information to accrediting bodies about students who

may be entitled to examination concessions, such as additional time, use of information and communications technology, and a reader or an amanuensis.

- Helping colleagues understand and support the special arrangements for exams that may be available and needed for SEN students.
- Careful planning and discussion of students' work experience placements to ensure inclusion of their personal needs, interests and strengths, which will have a direct influence on their confidence and self-esteem.
- The consolidation of cross-curricular links through key skills as described in the revised National Curriculum.
- Providing information to students and their parents or carers on public accreditation, which is realistic and flexible and may include combined programmes of GCSE, GNVQs, Award Scheme Development Accreditation Network (ASDAN), and other accredited pathways.
- Planning internal school accreditation through records of achievement, internal certification and the recognition and celebration of achievement.
- The offer of option support sessions which allow students to review and reinforce Programmes of Study; receive individual and small group support for coursework and general organisation, and revise basic skills, study skills and thinking skills.
- Providing opportunities to link review sessions directly with realistic personal targets and expectations for further accreditation or careers experience.
(Adapted from Cowne and Murphy 2000)

Discussion of differentiation and targets for IEPs

The last two chapters have looked at different aspects and models of differentiation. Curriculum arrangements are part of the School Improvement Plan. This will need to link to the school's SEN policy (see Chapter 2). SENCOs have a key role to play in helping to integrate these two policies.

Differentiation had become a 'buzz' word in the period after the passing of the Education Reform Act. By now the principle should be embedded in practice, as seen by Ofsted inspectors in their evaluation of lessons. Teachers, however, still need help in clarifying what the term means for them within their class or their subject. Differentiation is clearly about planning and organising tasks, resources and support, as well as about differentiating assessment modes or levels and providing feedback to the student about progress. But it is also about establishing learner-centred methods of delivery across the curriculum boundaries. The pupil increasingly should take control and learn to negotiate their own targets, take risks, and work with others on open-ended as well as prescribed tasks.

Individual Education Plans need to feed into the short-term lesson planning. Ideally, if this planning were done perfectly for every pupil, there would not need to be separate special needs paperwork. But if the IEP is to be effective it has to be flexible and incorporate different ways of conceptualising the learning process. For some skill-based areas of learning an objectives approach, using small steps, is most effective using the SMART targets. But for other areas of learning a more open-ended approach will be needed. As Norwich (1995) suggests, 'a broad and flexible attitude needs to be developed as to what is a target in an IEP'. He suggests that targets may be written as:

- specific objectives in observable learner outcome terms for which specific teaching strategies can be derived;
- sets of related and more general objectives linked to general teaching procedures, or learning outcomes based on general teaching principles with expected outcomes of only the most general kind. (p. 29)

Earlier in this same discussion paper, Norwich debates the idea that some areas and levels of learning cannot be isolated from each other and broken down into small detached linear steps. As discussed earlier in Chapter 4, alternative models may be needed which include a focus on creative and original outcomes, whether in cognitive or experiential areas of the curriculum. As Norwich concludes: 'this model calls for identifying learning encounters or processes without any specific pre-conceived ideas about outcomes'. He adds, 'the position taken on these issues will influence how you approach drawing-up IEPs'. It will also influence how schools develop their future curriculum, particularly as further flexibility is introduced through revised National Curriculum arrangements.

CHAPTER 6

Managing Effective Support

In recent years, the management of support systems has become a central role for SENCOs or senior staff in most schools. Many kinds of additional staff have been funded by the LEA or the school to support pupils with SEN. Most pupils with statements of SEN will have been allocated some support. This is often provided by Learning Support Assistants (LSAs), now called Teaching Assistants (TAs). Visiting teachers may offer advice or support for individuals or groups. Staff who are part of the school should be given clear job descriptions when joining the school. Induction training should also be available. The SENCO's role in relation to the coordination and management of support is likely to be significant. It could include the need to:

- hire, induct and manage support teams – in conjunction with the senior management team;
- establish the support needs of pupils and colleagues;
- arrange and support timetables;
- monitor support in relation to pupil progress;
- arrange liaison time for support teams and subject teachers, including liaison time with the SENCOs themselves;
- provide support personally to pupils or staff;
- organise staff development for support teams;
- build links with outside support services and agencies and liaise with them to ensure good partnership can occur;
- support individual parents through interviews and case conferences;
- keep the senior management team and governors informed of support issues and resource implications.

This description may seem daunting, but is based on observation of the work of many SENCOs. It becomes clear that in large schools, or those with many support staff, the management of support requires time and expertise if it is to be carried out effectively.

Health and safety issues

The health and safety of children and support staff should be carefully thought out as part of school policy. As it is likely that in many schools SENCOs will have responsibility for managing LSAs, this is an aspect they should address when employing, training and monitoring staff.

When a child with a statement is due to arrive and an assistant is hired, the health and safety procedures for the child must be planned. If necessary, professionals from the health service should advise on matters such as lifting, toileting or administering therapies. Support staff may need training to use specialist equipment. Administering medication must also be according to strictly agreed procedures, with permission from parents. LSAs should not normally be left in sole charge of children – if out of the classroom, they must know who is available to help and where this person can be found. Restraint training and procedures should also be covered where applicable, usually under LEA procedural advice.

Who may provide support?

The range of people who might be found working alongside a class teacher may include: LSAs working with statemented children, other teaching assistants employed by the school, i.e. learning support teachers – either those who are part of the school staff or peripatetic teachers/advisors from an LEA service, special school teachers working in an outreach capacity, and volunteers or parents.

It is possible therefore that there may well be one or more additional adults working in many classrooms. Pupils may also meet several support personnel across a week. Because of the potential complexity of support it is essential that there is a support policy which establishes some basic principles. Proper record keeping of visits and activities is also essential.

Provision mapping

Provision mapping can be a useful tool to track how the school's resources are being used, by recording details of the range of support given to children with SEN in each of the year groups. It assists costing and could reduce the bureaucracy of writing too many IEPs. Using this approach can also be linked to the 'waves of support' concept of the expanding National Literacy Strategy. Gross and Berger (2002) describe this approach in more detail. (See also Activity 4).

What is effective support?

What is considered to be effective support, and for whom? This could be:

- for the individual child;
- for groups of children;
- for curriculum differentiation or modification;
- for in-class teaching support.

To this list one could add support for the SENCO!

Pupils, with or without statements, will have IEPs which set targets. Part of the strategy to meet these targets may be to offer additional support from an adult: a teacher, LSA or occasionally a volunteer parent. This adult works alongside the child in class. Their role is to help the pupil be as independent a learner as possible. So they will check that instructions have been understood, keep the pupil on task by encouragement and praise, as well as add additional teaching points. This type of support is often given by LSAs and is particularly productive for younger pupils.

An additional teacher should be expected to do more than this. They should be helping plan the IEP for the child and may be teaching certain aspects directly. Sometimes, for very short periods, this extra teaching takes place outside the classroom in a withdrawal group. Sessions must be carefully planned to back up what is happening in class, and flexible timetabling will be needed so that pupils do not lose their curriculum entitlement. Small group work within class may be just as effective, although this depends on features of classroom organisation and space. In some rooms finding space for extra adults is a problem. For certain activities, especially those requiring careful listening, the class environment is too noisy. In other cases the group activity itself will be too disruptive to the rest of the class.

A lot has been said about the effects of withdrawal on the pupil's self-image. Younger pupils rarely mind being taken in a group because their need for extra attention is so great. With older pupils, it may be best to negotiate with the pupil and let them choose what sort of support they would like. Often a 'clinic' approach for such difficulties as spelling and reading can result in self-referral. This is effective for older pupils, especially when they are preparing coursework. The Ofsted (1996a) report found that withdrawal sessions were particularly effective in secondary schools in raising pupil standards.

Support for different groups

Adult support is most often given to small groups, even when the target child is the one for whom it was originally allocated. Pupils need time and space to attempt tasks, make and learn from mistakes and develop autonomy. An over-protective type of support will suppress independence. Children with the following difficulties are often given LSA support, monitored by specialists from agencies or advisory teachers from outside the school. Sometimes schools group pupils with similar needs and resource these by extra staff.

Physical difficulties (e.g. cerebral palsy)

The LSA's main aim will be to enable the pupil to be as independent as possible. It can be a complex role supporting those with severe physical disabilities. It is likely to involve carrying out physiotherapy, occupational therapy and possibly speech and language therapy under the guidance of visiting therapists. These programmes carried out by assistants and parents maintain the child's physical mobility. Visiting therapists monitor, assess and plan extensions of the programme but SENCOs should also keep good records of these visits.

Language and communication difficulties

Speech and language therapists in some health districts are beginning to train LSAs to work with them in teaching children with some of the less severe speech and language problems, which can be supported by school-based programmes. In such cases the SENCO may be responsible for ensuring both good teamwork and record-keeping.

Hearing impairment

LSAs employed to support those with hearing impairment may have learnt to sign where this is appropriate. They will work closely with the visiting teachers of the deaf who will advise on suitable ways to support the child within the curriculum.

Visual impairment

LSAs employed to support pupils who have significant levels of visual impairment often carry out specific tasks such as being responsible for enlarging worksheets. This requires advice from a visiting teacher for visual impairment who liaises with subject or class teachers. Some pupils will need to learn Braille, others will benefit from learning to type. LSAs have sometimes had special training to act as instructors for these skills.

Support for pupils with emotional or behavioural difficulties

The group of pupils with emotional or behavioural difficulties presents a different kind of challenge when planning. Clearly they too need access to the curriculum and help to overcome blocks to learning which arise from their internal state of anxiety or fear of risk-taking. Teachers too need a different quality of support when facing challenging or worrying behaviour, establishing classroom rules and building positive relationships. A behaviour policy for the school should not only be about rules, rewards and sanctions, but cover staff development and the support needs of teachers.

Hanko (1995) explores in depth how staff development groups working with an outside consultant or a specially trained member of staff can work together in a problem-solving mode. Building on her work in both primary and secondary schools, developed over a number of years, she explains the purpose of such staff groups. Each session focuses on a specific child and through sharing the knowledge of the teachers present and the skills they already possess, the group helps the teachers to find answers which will improve the situation and help the child cope better. Hanko says that by helping teachers realise the depth of knowledge they already possess about the learning process, the curriculum and child development, their objectivity is restored and confidence gained. She suggests that knowledge can be shared about the child, the whole classroom group in relation to the child, the teacher–pupil interaction and the therapeutic potential in the day-to-day curriculum.

The skills can be shared about:

- gauging the needs of a specific case from the behaviour displayed;
- making special bridging efforts to reach the child's 'teachable self';
- providing a consistent setting of new learning experiences likely to meet the needs gauged;
- if possible involving the child's parents and, if necessary, colleagues (fellow teachers and members of other professions) as genuine partners. (p. 62)

She further suggests that by working on the underlying issues, the whole group of teachers develop problem-solving skills which they can use in other cases.

Whatever individual or group support is available, it cannot compensate for a poorly differentiated curriculum. If the focus is solely on the child and not the curriculum and classroom content, this form of support may fail. This is, of course, one of the dilemmas of SEN: the tension between meeting individual needs and the requirements of accessing the core National Curriculum. The location for support need not be problematic, as long as it provides this access and ensures progress. *The task of the SENCO is to keep inclusive principles at the forefront of everyone's mind when planning the curriculum schemes of work, lesson plans and support timetables.*

Supporting the curriculum differentiation/ modification

This view of support can be seen as an additional means of ensuring that the curriculum is accessible to a wider range of pupils. It often takes the form of collaborative partnerships where two teachers plan and deliver aspects of the subject and where good use of group work is possible. It requires excellent joint planning to use the skills and knowledge of both teachers. The SENCO often acts in the role of support teacher as a means of helping develop good practice.

As the availability of teachers to offer direct support is being reduced, it is often the case that teaching support becomes advisory in nature. In schools where SENCOs have to support across large schools, their time may be best spent in helping their colleagues develop strategies for curriculum modification linked to pupils' IEPs. In many LEAs SEN specialist personnel are able only to act as advisors to school staff who will carry out the work on a daily basis. This partnership will involve joint planning for curriculum delivery or use of specialist resources or techniques.

Certain pupils will have needs which cannot be met within the school's normal resources of expertise. Such pupils will need support from visiting professionals who have specialist training and access to specialist or scarce resources, some of which they may provide or loan to the school. Knowing when to ask for such help, and from whom, is important for SENCOs. Pupils who may require such specialist support and advice are usually at *School Action Plus* of the Code of Practice (2001) or already have a statement for SEN. Such pupils include those with severe hearing impairment, visual impairment, physical impairment, or language impairment, severe literacy or learning difficulties, or emotional and social problems. Liaising with such specialists and keying their work into the school day and to the curriculum is another major role given to SENCOs. This will be explored further in Chapter 7.

LSAs can support the curriculum too, not by planning whole lessons, but by sharing ideas of how to follow up a theme or produce a resource. LSAs often say, during training sessions, that they are an underused resource: 'If teachers would only explain what they want the children to do – we could prepare better and get materials together.'

In my experience LSAs are very often frustrated by lack of clarity from teachers as to the curriculum goals to be reached. Prerequisite skills and concepts can be rehearsed with pupils prior to a lesson. This is often a very useful form of support. Specialist materials can also be produced by LSAs under instruction. Innovative ideas can be generated by assistants as long as these curriculum goals have been made clear to them *in advance* of the lesson delivery. Allowing the full potential of all in the team will benefit all of the children, but will require joint training, including the understanding of the importance of role definition.

Liaison time

Hart (1991) states that successful collaborative partnerships are made, not born, and are a product of continual careful negotiation. The classroom context is part of the experience that affects children's individual responses to learning. These are a product of the conditioning that goes on in classrooms. Hart (1995) argues that differentiating the curriculum to meet individual needs is also about understanding these classroom processes. She says:

> What we call individual differences are thus not objective descriptions of individual qualities and characteristics which exist independently of school and classroom contexts and the interpretative frameworks of teachers. They are products of school and classroom processes, not simply a natural reflection of inherent differences in children. (p. 38)

Working together, adults can help each other make sense of the complexity of the classroom environment. Successful teams will use time to analyse the various elements of classroom interactions and evaluate how support can best contribute to solving the various problems that arise. The problem is that time is scarce and rarely of sufficient quality to allow this to happen. Liaison time is often not seen as a priority by senior management.

It will therefore be an important part of the SENCO's role to fight for such time to be available for classroom teams to work together on a regular basis. Without liaison time, what could be the most effective way to support the curriculum and the child with SEN is ineffective and this considerable additional resource could thus be wasted.

Managing in-class support

This may not seem very different from the support for the curriculum, but perhaps is more to do with partnering, of a different kind. It occurs most when an LSA or a teacher works for large parts of the day in one class or where teaching support is otherwise available on a regular basis. Support is then seen as a resource which the teacher manages along with organisation of tasks and the physical resources of materials and space. From this point of view, the teacher is the room manager in charge of the team and as part of this managerial role deploys the time of extra adults to particular tasks. The teacher is supported if this room management is efficient and everyone knows their role.

For many teachers, having another adult in their classroom presents a threat to their control or a fear of criticism of their work. Even when both adults are happy to work together there are difficulties to overcome. The support teacher who is the 'outsider' may have to start by establishing their credibility. Preparing good materials and offering support with differentiation may be a start. Once 'entry' has been accepted, then working in a flexible way to support both the curriculum, the teacher and the child, or group of children, will begin. Ground rules about control, beginnings and ends of lessons and marking work, need to be established.

There are no set rules, each pair or team needs to work out what is best for their own context. The best partnerships recognise the different strengths of their members, and allow control of content, delivery and assessment to be shared. Teams which include LSAs need to recognise that some tasks are not appropriate to be given to the non-teacher. Such tasks would include whole-class teaching and unsupervised group work outside the classroom. LSAs, on the other hand, are very good at understanding children's emotional and social needs, preparing materials under guidance and carrying out well planned IEPs, if the strategies and targets have been explained. Secondary schools, particularly those with devolved funding, have recently increased their use of LSAs for support work to reduce costs. In such situations, it will be even more *important for the SENCO to establish policy guidelines and job descriptions for use of LSAs/TAs.*

Thomas (1992) found that the self-selecting teams of teachers, parents and assistants that he questioned in his research relied very heavily on an 'affective schemata'. A premium was placed on positive interpersonal relationships and unspoken understandings. Teachers could find other adults in their classes stressful. Their reaction to this was to reinforce their professionalism and defend their territory. Classroom support could, in these cases, have diminishing returns for pupils, if these stress reactions were too pronounced.

However, the opportunities that are presented by routine working partnerships are tremendous. Better differentiation and group work can take place. Learning can be better mediated by an adult working with the pupils to enhance thinking and language. *SENCOs should explain to senior managers that classroom teams need time to work out their respective roles and responsibilities and a way of working together.*

When the team is made up of two teachers, then it is possible to change roles occasionally: the class teacher becomes the supporter and the support teacher takes the whole class. Working with an individual or small group can then give the class teacher an opportunity to observe faulty strategies used by the pupils and to understand how better to intervene.

Training of Learning Support Assistants

Balshaw (1999) gives useful guidance on the training needs of LSAs. She lists some principles which should be addressed when planning a training programme. These include:

- establishing clear roles and responsibilities. This includes relationships to pupils, parents and teachers.
- gaining clear understanding of the communication systems of school and class.
- developing consistency of approaches towards positive provision.
- establishing ground rules for each team – valuing the assistants' work and not using them as 'dogsbodies'.
- offering support for personal and professional skill development.

To which I would add:

- understanding National Curriculum principles and assessment procedures in outline.
- learning principles about teaching reading, writing and mathematics.
- outlining key issues about managing behaviour.
- understanding different types of disabilities and learning difficulties.
- using IT to support learning.
- helping enhance self-esteem.

Fox (1998), Lorenz (1998) and Balshaw (1999) all emphasise the need to train LSAs and teachers together so that policies and practices for support move forward in a coherent manner. Misunderstandings over roles and responsibilities are much more easily sorted out by joint training. Balshaw (1999) gives examples of staff development exercises which will aid such joint training enterprises. Fox (1998) contains useful chapters for both LSAs and class teachers, explaining their work together.

The SENCO's role in relation to giving support

Many SENCOs work as a support teacher themselves for part of the week. This may be for a few lesson periods, or even a whole timetable that they can organise themselves. SENCOs are very experienced teachers and can have much to offer by way of help to pupils and their teachers. A secondary SENCO writes:

> The further you get away from the classroom the harder it is to give valid advice, so working part of the week with *hands-on experience,* keeps you up to date with materials and techniques and lends credibility when giving advice to colleagues.

However, it is important to be clear about roles. The SENCO's role is to co-ordinate the SEN work in the school. If they choose to deliver support for too much of the time this could leave too little time for their organisational and management work. Another important task is to encourage other teachers to differentiate the curriculum and organise the classroom so that the majority of needs can be met from within the normal resources of the school. The SENCO will be needed most for advice for those with more intractable and persistent needs. SENCOs have a role in helping assess pupils' needs and designing and reviewing IEPs with staff, especially at Stage 3 (Action Plus). This may require them to teach in order to get to know the pupil in his/her environment.

SENCOs must keep an overview of what is happening to support staff in their school. This means setting up a meeting system where the different groups can voice concerns, sort out problems about children or staff and generally feel supported themselves. Monitoring the success of support and its relationship to pupil progress is a vital role for SENCOs.

SENCOs may need to provide support to families

This is a much rarer way of conceptualising school-based support, but in fact a lot of school SEN time is spent in just this activity. It may be a useful way to support the child. Talking to parents of children with difficulties, finding out their concerns and worries and entering into agreements over goals, are all ways of supporting parents and through this, their children. Listening to parents and being aware of their anxieties is an important aspect of the SENCO's consultative role, which is explored further in Chapter 10.

Support for the SENCO

Who supports the supporter? For an effective SEN policy to work the SENCO needs support from senior management. They should report to a deputy head or be part of the senior management team. There are many decisions that need to be shared and communication between the SENCO and management is vital.

Many LEAs have SENCO network meetings at least termly. These meetings serve to support the work of the SENCO and to share ideas across the district. If this is not happening, perhaps a cluster of schools could get together to arrange meetings. They might make themselves into a branch of a national organisation such as NASEN (National Association of Special Educational Needs) (see Source List 2). They might use this to organise in-service training for themselves. Such networks of support give everyone opportunities to hear what others do, to problem-solve and to agree on local procedures and priorities. The SENCO Forum, set up by the National Council for Educational Technology, provides an Internet conference for subscribers and helps SENCOs from becoming isolated (see Source List 1).

Clerical support for SENCOs

The Code of Practice (2001) points out the value of allocating administrative staff time to help the SENCO, thus releasing the SENCO to use his or her expertise more effectively (6:10). This would come from funding devolved to schools for SEN. There are now also many commercial IT packages to help in the production of IEPs.

Training for SENCOs

Galloway (1985) and Hanko (1995) both emphasise that to meet the needs of children with learning and behavioural difficulties it is also necessary to meet the needs of their teachers. To address these 'teachers' needs' requires well targeted in-service training to help staff become more confident and competent. If the SENCO is to take a lead in this process they need training which focuses not only on knowledge but also on the consultation skills required to help others. As Hanko (1995) states, 'Such skills take time to develop and it requires support to practise them in the face of the range of complexities which confront special needs co-ordinators' (p. 140).

SENCOs themselves need access to longer training courses. The consultative document on National Standards for SENCOs issued by the Teacher Training Agency in 1998, lists key areas of SEN coordination. It follows that these would also be the key areas for SENCO training in the future. The key areas are:

(a) Strategic direction and development of SEN provision in the school.
(b) Teaching and learning.
(c) Leading and managing staff.
(d) Efficient and effective development of staff and resources.

It is acknowledged that the SENCO's role will largely depend on the head teacher's and governors' support reflected in school policies and practices. The TTA consultative document lists the professional knowledge that SENCOs should aim to understand (p. 12). It also lists the skills and attributes that SENCOs should aim to develop. The head teacher should ensure that their SENCO has access to specific training related to the development of these skills (p. 14).

Courses have been planned jointly by LEAs and Institutes of Higher Education to be funded by the TTA or from the Standard Fund (funds given by government for specific training requirements). It is worth making enquiries to local colleges and universities, and your SEN advisor or inspector. The Open University SENCO training is open to all who work in a school or college setting. Such courses will expand on all the issues raised in the chapters of this book. However, an important part of all training is the opportunity to meet fellow teachers and to share problems and ideas for their solutions. Opportunities to share ideas, learnt from training experiences, back in school with subject departments, year groups or class teachers will also need building into the school's staff development programme.

Reviewing support policies

This chapter has explored types of support and considered how to make support more effective. Several points emerge for SENCOs to remember. These are:

- Teachers and other adults working together in classrooms need training opportunities to develop good teamwork and communication.
- Policies need to include information about how support will be monitored to show pupil progress.
- Time for liaison and training must be allocated by senior management and governors as part of the school's SEN policy.
- On induction, support staff should have job descriptions and guidance notes. They also need a line manager, who is often the SENCO, with whom regular meetings are possible.
- SENCOs also need to consider their own time management and balance the various aspects of management of support, teaching children and training adults who support children.
- SENCOs themselves need access to support groups and training courses. Cowne (2003) gives examples of how SENCOs in training reviewed support policies as part of their course work.

SENCOs have a role in explaining the importance of these issues to the SMT and governors. If not addressed, a valuable resource may be wasted or not used efficiently for the benefit of the pupils. The Ofsted report (1996) *Promoting High Achievement for Pupils with SEN* stated that 'the most influential factor on the effectiveness of in-class support is the quality of joint planning of the work between class/subject teacher and the support teacher'.

Activity 5 may be used as an audit to check that the policy for learning support assistants is working. It can be adapted to cover other aspects of support work.

CHAPTER 7

Multi-professional Networks

This chapter looks at the partnership with bodies beyond the school and how this links to the school's SEN policy and practice as laid out in the Code of Practice (2001) (Regulation 3(1), Schedule 1, Section 3) (see Appendix 2b). As the SENCO Guide (DfEE 1997) states, it is important for SENCOs to spend time finding out about external agencies and services and what they can offer. Some LEAs provide lists for schools or organise cluster group meetings with multi-professional input. The SENCO's role is made much easier when the relevant agencies identify contact people and clear working practices.

> Such services include specialist teachers of pupils with hearing, visual, and speech and language impairments, teachers providing more general learning and behaviour support services, counsellors, educational psychologists, and advisers or teachers with knowledge of information technology for children with special educational needs. Curriculum support and advisory services can also be a resource for advice on specific subject-related teaching techniques and strategies and curriculum materials.
>
> (Code of Practice 2001, 10:7)

LEA duties

The LEA has a duty under the Code of Practice to inform schools of education services that are available and how these should be accessed and funded. LEAs must ascertain the demand for the SEN services from schools. Schools and their governors have responsibilities under the Code to identify, assess and make provision using LEA support services and/or health and social services as considered necessary. They must also publish the school's arrangements for working in partnership with those services.

LEAs must publish information about their policy on inclusion in their education department plans. The Programme for Action (DfEE 1998c) advises the dissemination of good practice by special schools in developing links with mainstream schools.

Whatever arrangements are made should be made explicit in the school's policy. Any extra responsibilities which this gives the staff in the school concerned also need to be clearly agreed and be written into the policy.

School Psychological Services

Each LEA in England and Wales has a School Psychological Service (SPS). Educational psychologists from the SPS often work a 'patch' system looking after a cluster of schools on a regular basis. They form an important resource for the school especially when they work there on a regular basis. Their role is often linked to providing assessment and advice for the statementing procedure. However, they can be invaluable when giving advice to teachers about pupil behaviour or other pupils causing concern. SPS often run projects to develop new strategies or techniques and support staff development.

Education Welfare Service (sometimes called Education Social Workers)

Education Welfare Officers (EWOs) are employed by the LEA to help parents and the LEA meet statutory obligations in relation to school attendance. They can play an important role with pupils who also have SEN, in helping liaise between home and school and maintaining communication in cases where attendance is sporadic. There are often underlying reasons for poor attendance which relate to learning or behavioural difficulties. Partnership between SENCOs and EWOs can be very productive in sorting out some of these underlying difficulties and easing a pupil back into school. EWOs can provide support and counselling for those children not in school or at risk of exclusion.

Child health services

Many District Health Authorities do not overlap geographically with LEAs. There may therefore be more than one health authority with which an LEA must communicate. The SENCO needs to know the relevant authority for their school. A school's first point of contact will be through the local school health service, whose professionals include speech and language therapists, occupational therapists and physiotherapists, community paediatricians, doctors and the school nurse. Local hospitals will also have a paediatric service in which physiotherapists and occupational therapists will work. Just how much hospital services can work with schools varies enormously from district to district.

Schools may consult health services with the parent's consent when wishing to check whether there is a medical condition which may be contributing to a child's difficulty in school.

If necessary, and with informed consent and involvement of the child's parents, a special medical examination can be requested. It is wise to check that hearing and vision, for example, have been examined. The school health service will have records of school aged children, especially if there are known special needs, which can be accessed as necessary.

Pupils on regular medication for conditions such as asthma, diabetes or epilepsy do not have special educational needs as such, but may miss some schooling. Certain pupils may have appliances which need to be maintained. An obvious example is hearing aids, which are usually checked by the LEA's hearing impaired service, who work in close cooperation with the Health Authority. Children with more severe disabilities will have been identified in early childhood by the Health Authority and the LEA will have been notified. General practitioners, however, are less likely to be aware of the Code of Practice. Child community health is the best source of information for schools.

Child and Adolescent Mental Health Services (CAMHS)

Some children and young people identified as having SEN may benefit from referral to CAMHS – specialists for assessment and treatment of mental health problems. CAMHS can also provide support and consultation to family members, carers and workers from health, social care, educational and voluntary agencies (Code of Practice 2001, 10:28).

Social Services

Social service departments should ensure that all schools in their area know the name of and how to contact the designated social services officer who has responsibility for pupils with SEN. Every child who is 'looked after' by the local authority must have a care plan which sets out their long-term objectives. This will incorporate the Personal Education Plan, giving any SEN arrangements (Code of Practice 2001, 10:37).

Not all such children will have SEN, so may not be the responsibility of the SENCO. Liaison within school between SEN and pastoral systems will be important in these cases. Campbell (1995) advises that schools need to know how to contact their designated officer from social services and of any referral format agreed by the social services department. The SEN policy needs to set out clearly the arrangements for working in partnership with social services and who on the school staff has responsibility for liaison, information collection and dissemination and individual planning which links to IEPs and Personal Education Plans.

The Connexions Service

This service will have the responsibility to work with all young people between the ages 13 and 19. The LEA must have in place arrangements for working in partnership with Connexions to ensure the needs of the young people are fully served.

(Code of Practice 2001, 10:14)

The service is delivered through a network of personal advisors linking in with specialist support services. The service will give greater priority to those young people at greatest risk (see also Chapter 8).

Voluntary organisations

Many disability groups have charities which concentrate on one impairment. The best known are organisations like the Royal National Institute for the Blind (RNIB), Invalid Children's Aid Nationwide (ICAN) and SCOPE (formerly the Spastics Society). All of these have set up specialist schools and training for specialist teachers. There are large numbers of smaller groups specialising in a wide range of disabilities. One of the key roles of voluntary organisations is to put parents in touch with others in the same situation as themselves. This, combined with factual information about the disability, is the most important way voluntary organisations can be used. The Council for Disabled Children publishes lists and contact numbers and can answer questions about a whole range of children's problems (see Source List 2). There are also local generic groups supporting parents and children with all types of SEN. Local addresses should be available from School Psychological Services (SPS) or the Education Officer for SEN. Parent Partnership Officers will also have contacts. SENCOs need to build up an information folder of local and national organisations, which includes named contacts with telephone numbers.

The DfES sponsors a network of eleven SEN Regional Partnerships. These bring together groups of local authorities and local health, social services, voluntary and private sector partners. The overall aim of the network is to secure greater consistency in the quality of the response to pupils with similar special educational needs.

(Code of Practice 2001, 10:39)

The SENCO's role in working within the multi-professional network

One of the SENCO's key roles is getting to know and working with the various support services and agencies that are available locally. There should be a file in the school giving basic information, including names and contact numbers, for all the agencies and services and how referrals can be made. It may be useful to include the addresses and contacts of special schools as they too have expertise and may be able to offer advice. The first task for a new SENCO is to see whether the school has this directory of services or an equivalent. Once the names and telephone numbers are known the next step is to get to know the individual contacts. The Code of Practice (2001) strongly suggests that SENCOs should have access to a telephone to fulfil duties related to networking with others. For the SENCO these could be the SEN Advisor; the Assistant Education Officer (Special); the Educational Psychologist; the teachers in the support services; the community health centre personnel; doctor and nurse. These will give access to a range of additional professionals, such as therapists. Added to this, there is a need to be aware of the voluntary organisations that have national networks and local branches or representatives. All of these services, agencies and organisations will work with parents, as will the school (see Figure 7.1).

The SENCO often plays a coordinating role for parents by putting them in touch with the multi-professional network, or by collating information from the various agencies who may work with the child and family. All parents have a key role to play with their children, especially those with SEN. Parents vary, from 'key workers' who have for years coordinated information about their child, to parents who are diffident and need encouragement to share decisions with the school.

The SENCO also has a key role in leading other staff and ensuring that appropriate in-service training is available regarding the various aspects of SEN, including working in partnership with those beyond the school.

Education	Health	Social Services
Educational Psychologists	Community Services School Nurse/Doctor Community Paediatrician	Children's services (sometimes part of generic services)
Education Welfare Officers	Child Care Officers	
Education Officer (statements) equivalent		
Parent Partnership Officer		
Advisory Teachers for SEN	Hospital Paediatrician	Disability Services or part of generic services
Teachers for the: Hearing impaired Visually impaired Language impaired Physically impaired	Specialist Doctors (hospitals) Speech & Language Therapists Occupational Therapists Physiotherapists	
Portage service for pre-school children	Health Visitors (pre-school) Assessment Centres	
Nursery schools and classes		Day nurseries (most private/voluntary)
Behaviour Support Services	CAMHS	
Pupil Referral Units		
Home Tuition Service		
Hospital Teachers		

Figure 7.1 Support services and agencies linked to SEN work

Getting to know key workers from health/social services

Because the focus of work of health or social service personnel is different from that of the school they will have different priorities. This will affect their management of time and whom they perceive as the client. It may be difficult to obtain support for teachers and the school when it is the child or family that in their view should receive their expertise. One way to overcome potential professional barriers is to get to know the individual worker on an informal basis outside of the case conference or meeting situation. Inviting professionals to school staff meetings to explain their roles and share ideas with teachers can be very helpful. Joint working practices can then be decided and then, when there is a problem to be solved, this joint understanding will lead to better results. The school nurse, for example, is a resource that is undervalued in many schools. Therapists and other health and social work professionals may also be persuaded to visit schools on a one-off basis as part of an awareness training session.

Defining the purposes of contributions from outside services and agencies

Once information about what is available locally and how it can be accessed is known, the next step for SENCOs is to define the purposes for which these outside agencies and services might be useful. Both the health and the education services will:

- Carry out assessments as part of the statutory process after a request from the LEA for Appendix reports towards the statementing process (see Appendix 9a).
- Support parents and families, particularly those undergoing statutory assessments. Support to parents may include helping those with attendance problems.
- Give advice and support to pupils with a range of disabilities.
- Provide direct therapies (speech and language, occupational or physiotherapy) or specialist support or teaching, including provision and use of specialist equipment, IT, etc. For this to be effective, advice needs to contribute to classroom practice and access to the National Curriculum.
- Contribute to case conferences and annual reviews of pupils.

Effective partnership between services and schools

As Diamond (1995) states:

> It is essential that the providers of SEN services to schools can articulate for themselves what characterises their distinctive contribution to the identification, assessment and making of provision in schools. Services can be agents of change but only if they work with a preventative role. (p. 65)

Diamond also suggests this will only be the case if the LEA support services can:

- support SENCOs in their work as 'a critical friend';
- remain practical at a classroom level, enskilling teachers with strategies to support SEN;
- help embed delivery of support by working within the National Curriculum and by seeing the IEP as an extension of normal classroom planning cycles;
- provide school-focused and school-based in-service training to staff;
- remain flexible to the needs of SENCOs and staff.

Each service will have a specialism and if possible this should guide the school's choice. Some learning support services and psychologists may have a range of specialists in their teams. Referrals to the service may initially be through the regular key worker, but that person will often know someone else who can help in special cases. Educational psychologists usually have good contacts with health and social services and may be the first contact for many referrals. On the other hand, some specialist services, e.g. hearing and vision, prefer direct contact. It is up to each service to make the referral routes clear to schools and parents.

From the above it is clear that, as part of their SEN policy, schools need to develop their procedures for referrals and requests to support services and agencies. Where there are a number of possible choices, decisions need to be made about the best route for support and advice. Over-referral to a number of agencies at one time, for the same case, is ineffective and wasteful of scarce resources.

The school/service working relationship

Certain support services may visit on a regular basis, others only on one-off occasions. Where the service is regular it is good practice to set up a contract or service level agreement. This is essential if the service is one which is bought in from delegated funds. This should state the priority for the work over the next term and list the names of pupils who will receive the advice or support. Such contracts should note how other agencies would be working in relation to the named pupils. Clear definitions of purpose should be made and very clear descriptions agreed about what the service will provide and how the school will support this delivery. This could be by providing sensible space to work or some resources. Time available from the service to the school should be clearly stated so that both sides fulfil their promises. For example, the school must inform the service in good time of closures or special events such as field trips which would make the delivery to a particular child impossible. The service must give information where possible of changes of day or time and of illness of the worker. Such agreements are common for school psychological services and learning support services of various kinds.

Other services expect to be 'on call', but will appreciate as much notice as possible. If one teacher, for example, works across a whole LEA they will have a full diary. Ample planning is needed to prepare reports for annual reviews. These are needed in good time for circulation before the meeting. It will be important to have clear procedures for services signing in or otherwise registering their presence in the school. SENCOs will need to know who has visited and for what purpose.

Keeping a record of service provision

It is also important in school to keep a record of who has been asked to help for any one child. This should be part of the paperwork attached to the IEP. It is good practice to have a top sheet in each file listing outside agency involvement (including dates) and indicating if a report is attached. Such a top sheet should be used from the early stages of the staged assessment process, so a cumulative record is kept (see Appendix 9b). Communication within the school about referrals is vital, especially when some services are used by the pastoral systems, and other services by the learning support department. There are cases where, for example, a pupil is excluded but the SENCO is not asked to contribute what is known about the pupil's difficulties. If outside services or agencies are given referrals by a school, the parents or guardian must be informed and in the majority of cases give permission. Services can support staff rather than the pupils, in which case parental permission would be inappropriate.

Statement support

In many LEAs support for statements has been delegated to schools. When this happens, the school receives a certain sum of money and must purchase or provide support for the pupil in accordance with the statement. They may wish to buy in advice from specialist teachers, either from the LEA or, where available, from independent services or those attached to charities. Such service provision will be paid for from delegated funds and must be carefully recorded and monitored as part of the pupil's annual review.

Services working collaboratively with teachers and SENCOs

The overwhelming demand from teachers, when getting outside advice and support, is for strategies to meet the IEP targets which are manageable within the normal structure of daily teaching. Some services, though excellent for carrying out assessment and teasing out any within-child factors causing a problem, may not direct support to teachers or SENCOs. An understanding of the curriculum and the social context of the classroom and school are also needed if staff are to be fully supported in meeting the needs of more complex individuals. Teachers may need to borrow equipment for a short time to try it out and many will need training about how it should be used. IT can help so many pupils with SEN, but knowing which equipment or software to buy and whether it will fit the pupils' needs requires expertise. Over time schools develop this expertise themselves, but it is useful to have specialist teachers who can give advice about matching resources to pupil needs. The SENCO should keep tracks on the extra resources provided or borrowed and be accountable for their efficient use.

Writing effective advice

For schools, the best professional advice is that which helps to contribute to the child's IEP in a practical way. For pupils with statements, the advice in the Appendices will have informed the statement writer, who will have then listed the needs and priority objectives for the school to achieve. (For appendices list see Appendix 9a.) On receipt of such a full statement in the new form, targets must then be set by the school, which will be reviewed at the annual review. If the report from the professional is full of jargon and results of tests unknown to the school, this is not helpful. It will be necessary to enquire of the report writer:

- What will this do to help us in the classroom?
- What is reasonable to expect of this pupil?
- How will we know if the result is sufficient and whether the targets have been reached (i.e. success criteria)?

Joint problem-solving sessions

There are a number of puzzling pupils for whom it isn't quite clear what is needed. Often the best way to support these pupils most effectively will be to enhance their teacher's own professional skills in the management of the class. If a visiting professional can find time for a joint problem-solving session with a group of staff, they can together elicit the information already known and produce questions which then can be followed up in an assessment. This will give the staff some strategies to try themselves, as well as providing added focus on the type of further information needed and from whom it could be expected. Such sessions make use of the scarce professional's expertise and help teachers to realise they may already have answers to their questions. These problem-solving sessions, in year groups for example, may be the best way SENCOs and support colleagues can develop IEPs. As the Audit Commission (1992) states:

> Success of support teams should not always be measured only by pupil progress. Schools may require both direct and indirect support and general guidance. Evaluation should take account of any role in increasing schools' capacities for managing pupils with SEN. (Par. 86, p. 55)

Therefore, services will be at their most effective if they can be seen to increase the school's capacity for meeting SEN. This means services must meet teachers' as well as the child's needs. If a teacher feels supported by knowledge that she or he is doing the right thing and can see the pupil taking a full part in school life and making progress, this will have been a piece of effective support. If, on the other hand, the expert advice has puzzled, confused or de-skilled the teacher, support will not have been so effective.

Parents as part of the multi-professional network

Parents need to know about outside services and agencies and have their various roles explained, especially if there is multi-agency involvement. Again this is best done informally, before the parent has to face a room full of strangers at an annual review or a case conference. Parents themselves will often be the SENCO's best source of information. If the child has been known to the health service since pre-school years, then the parent will know key workers from the community health services or the hospitals who have already worked with the child and provided advice.

In very complex cases the child may be known to up to 30 or so professionals. So for such complex disability cases the parent often is the key worker for their child, linking the therapies and advice together into an individual plan. Notes will be kept by each service in their files, but it is the parent who has the total picture. In cases where, for example, three therapists require programmes of practice at home, there may not be time for the 'just ten minutes' practice from school as well. The overarching purpose for support should be to support the teacher or parent to support the child. School support services cannot focus on the parent's adult needs, but they can help parents to support their children.

Strategic policy planning

One of the elements of the strategic development of policy and practice given in the TTA (1998) Standards document is the liaison with and coordination of the contribution of external agencies. This may include the interpretation of specialist assessment data and its use to inform practice.

It is probably at the stage of *School Action Plus* that the SENCO's role in working collaboratively with colleagues and support services becomes most important. SENCOs need to be proactive in planning IEPs for pupils by getting to know which will be the appropriate outside agency for the process.

This chapter has described in some detail the complexity of working within a multi-professional network. SENCOs will need to develop their own style of working which fits the context of their school and LEA. What is available will vary from district to district. Internal school organisation also varies enormously. In some schools, heads and senior managers deal with the outside agencies, in others it is the SENCO. Whatever the system, communication will be the key issue if the SENCO is to carry out their role effectively.

CHAPTER 8

Working in Partnership at Transition Periods

The SENCO needs to take a strong lead in helping colleagues to plan both entry and departure from the school for pupils with SEN. These are key points in the pupil's life: good planning, record-keeping and communication can make a great deal of difference to their well-being. There are three critical action times:

- *Entry to school* – planned entry is necessary for children identified in pre-school as having special educational needs, with or without a statement.
- *Transition between phases or schools* – usually primary/secondary although infant/junior or first/middle possible.
- *Leaving school* – for college or adult life. This involves the transition plan for pupils with statements but should be planned for all pupils with identified SEN.

All of these can involve working in a multi-disciplinary partnership. School policies should include a section where transfer procedures and the roles and responsibilities related to flow of information are made clear.

Early years and entry to school

Certain children have their special needs identified shortly after birth or before they are two or three years old. Health professionals will have taken the lead in this identification process and will have informed the LEA, who then can carry out multi-professional assessments for a statement and will do so for those whose needs warrant this and when the parent agrees.

Education offers some services pre-school – usually a Portage home visiting service which works directly with parents using a developmental checklist to identify the next learning step. Services of hearing and vision also make home visits as soon as the disability is diagnosed. Information about local provision for suitable placement for those with disabilities can be obtained from the local Children's Information Services (CIS). Parents should be encouraged to make contact with their local Early Years Development and Childcare Partnership (EYDCP). Planning entry to school from this variety of provision requires good liaison from all concerned. Usually some joint planning has taken place with the SENCO or class teacher, using the knowledge gained by the personnel who will have worked with the child and family before school entry. Many LEAs have an under-fives multi-disciplinary panel which can give advice about a child's needs to the receiving school.

There are important issues about entry to school for these more vulnerable children. Arrangements need to be flexible and an offer of gradual entry into the full-time experience of school life should be available. Parents have a vital role to play in this planned entry. The Code of Practice (2001), Chapter 4, shows clearly how the graduated response to identifying and assessing those with SEN should be used in early years settings.

This means that some children may have been placed on *Early Years Action* or *Early Years Action Plus* in their early years setting and the IEP may be in place on entry to school. This planning should help to build on what has already been done and help shape a smooth transition to school. It is therefore essential that good use is made of pre-school records when planning to build on existing achievements. Teachers should read and use the Foundation Stage records and other information available from all sources, including information from parents.

Disability Rights Commission Code of Practice (2002)

The DRC Code of Practice (2002) explains the duties of the responsible body (governors in the case of maintained schools). This Code gives examples of what can be considered as reasonable. As the duties are anticipatory the implication is that admission policies themselves must not be discriminatory. When the responsibility for the child changes the statement must be transferred to the new LEA. The new LEA may place a child in a different school from that named on the statement prior to amendment or re-assessment. Parents must be informed within six weeks of transfer when the statement will be reviewed and whether the LEA will make a re-assessment (Chapter 8, Code of Practice 2001). Part 4 of the statement will always need changing if a child moves to another school in the same LEA because of a change of address or a phase change.

It is important that all who teach the child are informed of the child's special educational needs. Schools must review the child's progress during the course of the year using normal curriculum and pastoral arrangements as well as IEPs. Although the Code does not specify this in detail the assumption is that the same good practice applies to pupils who have been placed on *School Action* or *School Action Plus*. Parents should be informed by the old school that records will be passed on to the new school including details of IEPs where appropriate.

Transfer to secondary school

The learning environment in secondary schools is different from primary settings in many ways. For example, in the primary school the child has a much clearer idea of what is expected by his or her teacher. In a primary school most lessons are taught by the class teacher; in the secondary school the pupil is taught by many different teachers who will not be as familiar with their special educational needs.

There is more movement around the school which may put the pupil with some SEN at a disadvantage because they will have to carry and organise their equipment. Therefore, the planning for pupils transferring to secondary schools must be very carefully executed. Visits should be made to acclimatise the pupil to the new building and meet some of the teachers, especially the SENCO. Make sure all records, including SEN records, are up to date and are transferred early enough in the summer term for those who need to know about the pupil's individual needs.

The school organising the departure needs to make personal contact with the new school wherever possible. A planning meeting, either at an annual review for a pupil with a statement, or an IEP review for others, should include parents and if possible someone from the new school. Support services have a vital role in transition by helping the new school make plans. Often, the same support teacher may be able to work with the pupil in the new school, but even when this is not possible another member of their team may do so. The receiving school must read all records in good time so that plans are in place before entry, especially for the more vulnerable pupils. This is usually well done for those with sensory or physical disabilities as support services and health personnel typically plan what equipment is needed and discuss mobility issues. Planning for pupils with more general difficulties is often much weaker. Yet for these pupils poor preparation may result in a setback to learning or in extreme cases such a traumatic start to the new school that the pupil never settles. In some schools members of the learning support department visit all tutor groups in the first two weeks of the new school year, in order to meet pupils with SEN and draw up a 'pen picture' of those learning characteristics which all staff need to know.

Transition plans at 13+

The Code of Practice (2001), Chapter 9, describes transition plan meetings which are usually held as part of the regular annual review meetings organised by the school. The responsibilities for running annual reviews and writing transition plans for those in year 9 and above are made very clear.

> The Transition Plan should draw together information from a range of individuals within and beyond school in order to plan coherently for the young person's transition to adult life. Transition Plans when first drawn-up in year 9 are not simply about post-school arrangements, they should also plan for on-going school provision, under the statement of SEN as overseen by the LEA. (Code of Practice 2001, 9:51)

The head teacher must invite the agencies that may play a major role in the young person's life during post-school years and must invite the Connexions Service. Parents' and young people's views must be sought. The Code of Practice (2001) describes what should be addressed by transition plans (9:51–9:69).

Russell (1995) states that the challenge of the transition plan lies in

- development of continuity of assessment,
- review and programme planning from school through further educational, vocational and personal preparation for a valued and productive adult life;
- coordination of the many different agencies and professions which can contribute to this process;
- the creation of positive approaches to participation by students and parents in assessment and planning for transition;
- the transfer of information and expertise between phases and agencies involved in transition;
- the provision of advocacy and advice directly to young people at a time of major changes in their family life and educational experience. (p. 58)

The Code of Practice makes it very clear that the young person must be actively involved in the development of the transition plan and their views taken into account. As Gascoigne (1995) points out, this may be the first time that the young person is consulted without parents being present. She suggests that parents may find this period very stressful as their feelings are ambivalent. 'On the one hand they want their child to become as independent as possible, and on the other, they wish to extend their protection of them' (p. 138). Both Gascoigne and Russell emphasise how sensitive parents can be and how much support they will need from those working with them.

Transition plans start in Year 9 and continue annually until the young person leaves school. It is important that all professionals involved build good relationships with the young person and their families and give them all information about what is available in their local area. The process is usually carried out very thoroughly in special schools, but should be available to pupils with SEN in mainstream schools.

LEAs must seek information from social services departments under Section 5 of the Disabled Persons (Services, Consultation and Representation) Act 1986, as to whether a young person with a statement under Part IV of the Education Act 1996 is disabled (and so may require services from the local authority when leaving school). (Code of Practice 2001, 9:58)

Children who have been looked after by the local authority until their 16th birthday will have a care plan and there will be a Connexions personal advisor (PA) for these young people. The care plan fulfils the same function as the transition plan. The Connexions service is responsible for overseeing the delivery of the transition plan, and the Connexions PA should coordinate its delivery. Details are provided in the *SEN Toolkit* Section 10 (see also paragraphs 9:63 and 9:64 of the Code of Practice 2001).

Post-16 transfer to colleges

In order to help young people and parents and carers, as well as school SENCOs, support staff and other key personnel, it may be useful to compile a handbook which will include simple, straightforward information about applying for college courses offered, and other practical considerations such as claiming disability living allowance.

Colleges should be approached with a view to including entry criteria for all courses in their prospectuses, including GNVQ Foundation and NVQ1, not just those where the needs of the accrediting body demand it. Admission to courses would then be based on fair and transparent procedures, and not on assumptions or subjective impressions. Colleges would benefit when planning provision, from year-on-year projections of those with specific types of disabilities. A high level of support in FE is needed for students with statements. Supported wheelchair access and supported physical care facilities may be required. Many other access issues must also now be considered, especially under the DRC Code of Practice for Post 16 (DRC 2002b), which states that colleges have a duty not to discriminate against those with any kind of disability in their admissions procedures.

There is a need to make improvement in the level of training for both FE lecturers and learning support staff on issues relating to SEN and disability. The Further Education Funding Council (FEFC) now provides staff development materials in response to the findings of *Inclusive Learning* (The Tomlinson Report, FEFC 1996).

The further education world is very competitive, and as colleges become able to recruit higher ability students, market demand may lead to a phasing out of some current courses for SEN students. Restricted funding of colleges means that students with more severe disabilities will need additional support from the FEFC. Moreover, the remit of the health service to work with students needing adult level health care is confined to schools.

As a result of the Learning and Skills Act (2000) a national learning and skills council was set up for England. This council has a duty to have regard to the needs of people with difficulties and disabilities and to provide equal opportunities for disabled and non-disabled people. This Act, in conjunction with the DRC and its Post 16 Code of Practice (2002) and the SEN Code of Practice (2001), gives a strong policy base for good practice to be developed in FE colleges.

Connexions Service

Transition planning using the Connexions Service will be key to effective planning of further education provision. However, it is vital that the information gathered reaches all who are involved in the enrolment of students. The Connexions Service will also be used as a bridge from schools or college to work placements (in the early stages of development at present).

It must be remembered that the young persons' views are all-important. Sometimes they do not want attention to be drawn to their differences by having individual support. Their permission must be sought before information is shared with staff. Personal plans with goal setting are now required for all Key Stage 4 students at potential risk of social exclusion, linked to a looser Key Stage 4 curriculum.

Under 16 students

Colleges are reporting that there is an increase in under sixteen year old students being transferred from schools, often for those with difficult to manage behaviour. Very careful planning will be required for these vulnerable younger students. As Sproson (2003) explains, successful placement in a college environment depends on the student's participation in the referral process, good preparation and the suitable appointment of a support liaison advisor. He further advises that FE placement will not be a suitable option for all such students.

CHAPTER 9

Managing Paperwork and Procedures: the Coordinating Role

This chapter links with Chapter 3 on identification and intervention and looks at the coordinating role of the SENCO in relation to the paperwork and procedures required by the Code of Practice (2001). The SENCO usually takes responsibility for managing their school's record-keeping system for all those with SEN and takes a lead role in organising the reviews of IEPs and annual reviews for those with statements. The Code of Practice has made great demands on SENCOs in terms of resources of time and their management abilities. This chapter describes ideas gathered from practice about ways of organising paperwork, holding reviews and setting targets for pupils with SEN in partnership with pupils, parents and colleagues. The chapter also describes special situations in which SENCOs might be asked to help prepare evidence for (a) SEN tribunals and (b) Ofsted inspections.

All of the above should be reflected in how roles and responsibilities are allocated and evaluated as part of the school's SEN policy as described in Chapter 2. One of the issues for large schools, particularly in the secondary phase, is how much of this responsibility can reasonably or efficiently be given to the SENCO and how the SENCO will communicate with others – particularly those in the pastoral team, the head and governors.

The work described here is perceived as an important part of the coordinating role, though not necessarily to be carried out by the SENCO alone. The head has the ultimate responsibility to see that these tasks are carried out effectively and in turn must report to the governors on their effectiveness.

The tasks required include:

- the management of IEP reviews for those on school-based stages and those with statements usually on a termly basis but at least twice a year;
- holding annual reviews for pupils with statements; this is the responsibility of the head teacher but in practice is often delegated to the SENCO; in any case, both head and SENCO need to know the procedures;
- organising paperwork for a request for multi-disciplinary assessments;
- contributing to the educational advice for the statutory assessment when requested by the LEA;
- setting targets within two months of receipt of the statement – designing an IEP for each pupil with a statement in conjunction with relevant staff;
- supporting the head if she or he is requested to attend a tribunal, by helping prepare paperwork;
- supporting the head in preparing paperwork for an Ofsted inspection;
- contributing to the review of the whole-school policy for SEN or a section on SEN in the School Development Plan.

All of the above will require organisation skills and clarity of purpose and call on interpersonal skills when involved in dealing with a range of people: the child, parent, teacher and other professionals. This consultative work will be covered in more depth in the next chapter. This chapter will concentrate on the organisational and bureaucratic aspects of the work.

Organisation of files

It may sound mundane or even trivial but a lot rests on how and where files are stored, and how accessible these are to the SENCO and staff alike. There is no single correct way to do this, each school needs to decide on a system which works for them and then to make it clear within their policy document. The following are examples of ways it could be done.

- Have one filing system in the school office with a subsection in each file labelled SEN (or colour coded). This will work if the filing system is both accessible to relevant staff and visiting professionals but is secure. It will not work if the room is locked when office staff leave in the evening and the teachers and SENCO cannot gain access.
- Have a separate SEN register filing cabinet in the SENCO's room which is accessible to teachers and visiting professionals as is relevant. This means the main file also needs marking to indicate there is a SEN file elsewhere. Duplication of the file is likely to be expensive. It makes a segregated record system which may be difficult to cross-reference.
- Use a computerised system of records which link to IEP commercial packages (see Source List 1 for examples).
- Devolve all SEN filing to class teachers/year departments, and ask them to write IEPs and review them. Then the role of the SENCO will be to monitor the process. It would be wise, however, to keep a management form to collate information about the number of schools a child has attended, guardian names, number of outside professionals involved and dates of reviews (see Appendix 9b for an example). This system would still need to be checked by the SENCO, who is responsible for seeing reviews are held and paperwork kept in order. The SENCO cannot distance themselves too much from the review process, particularly at *School Action Plus* where they have a key role to play. Consideration should be given to using SEN funding to give clerical support to SENCOs as is now recommended in the Code of Practice (2001).

The management of the SEN records

The SEN record should contain, as a minimum, the list of names of pupils at each of the stages of the Code of Practice. Many schools keep other information on this register, such as short notes about the type of SEN each pupil may have, if English is their second language and the date of the last IEP review. Ofsted inspectors will also request to see SEN records along with other paperwork for SEN. Monitoring the SEN register and checking how representative it is across classes, gender and ethnic groups will expose any undue bias.

Organisation of IEP reviews

Of all the aspects of the Code of Practice, this is the most challenging to schools. Running these reviews is very time consuming for the class or subject teacher as well as for the SENCO. If parent and pupil views are to be fully incorporated, this too makes enormous demands on a school's resource of time. The number of pupils who require IEP reviews has risen. Careful thought should be given when deciding who needs an IEP. The Code of Practice (2001) suggests that only those with significant additional needs should have IEPs. Group IEPs may also be solutions for those with the more commonly occurring difficulties.

The whole strength of the graduated response depends on this review process being regular, thorough, and properly recorded. Teachers are complaining about the level of bureaucracy involved and saying it doesn't benefit themselves or their pupils. It is up to schools to develop ways which work for teachers and pupils, while still complying with the main principles of the Code of Practice. These are to identify and meet the needs of all pupils with any special need and to give them full access to the curriculum and life of the school. Good assessment makes for good teaching, so the IEP process must work to improve teaching and learning outcomes.

The IEP as a process of continuous assessment

There is much debate in schools about what constitutes an IEP. It clearly must be envisaged as a process and a set of documents. Writing one beautiful plan will not suffice; it is the setting and evaluating of the targets *over time* that makes an IEP valuable to the pupil. The key questions are:

- What does *this* pupil need as a priority to help them make progress in the curriculum? What are the pupil's and the parents' views?
- What level has the pupil already reached? (state existing levels of attainment, particularly in literacy and numeracy, in as precise a way as possible). What can the child do? What are their strengths?
- What are the logical next steps to be achieved within the priority areas chosen (i.e. set targets)? These need to be decided with the pupil wherever possible.
- How will the information from the IEP inform lesson planning by the teacher?
- How will these targets be achieved? Describe strategies and resources required, including frequency and timing of support.
- How will the targets be evaluated to see if they have been achieved?
- What will be the method of evaluation or assessment? This will help the review process. If the targets are not set in precise enough terms, it will be impossible to know if they were or were not achieved.

Decide who will monitor all of the above and how progress will be recorded.

At the review, check which targets are reached, which are partially reached and which have not been possible and then set new targets. These could be the same ones again, with different success criteria; or they could be new targets, depending on what was perceived as success and what had been difficult. The conditions under which success was achieved need to be stated. If the pupil only made progress when given support in class or through a specific programme of intervention, these strategies need to be noted.

IEP reviews also need to be held regularly, probably twice a term, for pupils with statements. Some may be 'mini reviews' with the support teacher and class teacher only, others may require the SENCO or parents to be present. The targets for pupils with statements will have been set first within two months of receipt of the statement or as part of the annual review process. The Code of Practice (2001) suggests that IEPs should be in place for all pupils with statements.

Holding a School Action Plus review to consider requesting a multi-professional assessment

Many pupils can remain at *School Action Plus* for some time, but this stage is characterised by the involvement of outside support services and agencies so it is unlikely that there will be resources available for many pupils to be at this stage for more than a year or so. Every effort should be made to help the pupil return to *School Action* once sufficient progress is made or suitable means of access to the curriculum provided. For those few pupils whose needs justify further assessment, careful and detailed documentation will be needed about their problems and how these have been met to date.

At the *School Action Plus* review, where a multi-disciplinary assessment is being considered, parents' views must be sought and the purpose explained in detail. The possibility that the LEA (a) may not agree to the making of the assessment, or (b) may not issue a statement after examining the outcome, must be explained along with the parents' right to appeal.

The professional who has been involved should contribute to this review. They will be asked for evidence as part of the assessment and their views are needed in this review. Parents can make a request for a multi-professional assessment independently of the school or support services, but the school continues to be required to give evidence.

Most LEAs have set quite stringent criteria for requests for statutory assessments which they will have published. LEAs often have proformas they wish schools to complete when requesting a formal assessment. The Code of Practice states very clearly that it is the head teacher's responsibility to make the decision to request a formal assessment, unless a parent has already done so. However, this is usually done in close cooperation with the SENCO. The LEA will need evidence of the pupil's needs and about what the school has already done to meet these. Copies of IEPs and reviews must be sent, with a summary paragraph stating why a statutory assessment is requested.

Schools will be asked to write the Educational Appendix as their contribution to the formal assessment process. All the advice will be attached to the draft statement and will be part of the document known as the statement (see Appendix 9a).

Contributions to school's advice for a statutory assessment (Appendix B)

Part A

Background information and context

Give a brief description of the school/setting and organisational and curricular arrangements. Give information about how long the child has been in your school and when the difficulties were first noted. Summarise, with dates, the child's movement through school-based stages, identify outside agencies' involvement and any support/provision given by the school to date. The parents' and child's views must also be recorded.

Current functioning

Give a description of the child's current skills and attainments. Identify skills in each area, giving National Curriculum levels where appropriate. Describe areas of strength as well as difficulties. Use headings such as reading, numeracy, and language development. Include descriptions of learning style and response to teaching. Describe behaviour, social skills, independence, self-help skills and the child's relationship to adults and peers. It could be useful to consider the areas of need given in the Code of Practice (2001) 7:52:

- communication and interaction
- cognition and learning
- behaviour, emotional and social development
- sensory, and/or physical.

Other factors

In this section mention any other factors such as attendance or medical history that might be relevant. Summarise relationship with family and parents' perceptions of the child's needs. Parents will be asked by the LEA to give their views in full in other appendices.

Part B

Special educational needs

Summarise on the basis of the above information your perception of the pupil's strengths and special educational needs. Be as specific as possible.

Part C

Aims of provision

Identify what you perceive would be the long-term aim of any provision given to the child by a statement. Link these aims to each need identified in Part B.

Part D

Comment on facilities and resources which you believe the child will need to fulfil the aims identified in Part C. Finally, include equipment (e.g. IT), ideas about differentiation/modification or support. Who would monitor these arrangements?

While an assessment is taking place the pupil continues to remain at *School Action Plus* and have IEPs written and reviewed as before. Under the Code the LEA is required to complete their assessment within six months. Their decision can be to make a statement with or without resources, or to issue a 'note in lieu'. In the latter case the pupil returns to *School Action Plus*, but with the information from the note to inform teachers of the pupil's needs. The other appendices to the statements come from parents, doctors, psychologists and other services (see Appendix 9a). (Further advice can be obtained from the *SEN Toolkit* (2001) Section 8.)

Setting targets on receipt of a final statement

When the school receives the final statement, they have two months in which to set targets for the first year and to send a copy of these to the LEA. In practice, schools need to develop IEPs for pupils with statements. These will be largely concerned with putting the targets into practice. Pupil views will need to be recorded and a careful record kept of how targets are evaluated. These targets will need to be reviewed regularly, and all those who teach the pupil kept informed of the revised targets. In large schools this will require a system to both collect, collate and share information to and from the learning support team.

All of this will contribute to the annual review where parents' and professionals' viewpoints will also be collected and where new targets will be set.

Annual reviews

The full details of annual review procedures are published in Chapter 9 of the Code of Practice (2001). Every child who has a statement of SEN must have this statement reviewed by the LEA at least annually. The Code of Practice (2001) states that

> The purpose of the annual review is to integrate a variety of perspectives in the child's progress and amend the statement to reflect newly identified needs and provision. The annual review should focus on what the child has achieved as well as on any difficulties that need to be resolved. (Code of Practice 9:4)

To do this, the LEA requires the head teacher to submit a review report by a specified date. The LEA will serve a notice to the school listing the pupils with statements and asking for a report on each. In order to prepare this review report, the head teacher must seek written advice from the parents, any professionals specified by the LEA, and anyone else the head teacher considers appropriate.

The head may delegate responsibility for running the review meeting, but must ensure that the teacher knows of all who should be invited.

What must be done in advance of the review date?

At least two months in advance of the meeting the head must request written advice from:

- the child's parents
- those the LEA has specified
- those the head teacher considers appropriate.

These are likely to be the class and support teacher or assistant, any specialist teacher giving advice or an educational psychologist, any health and social service professionals involved with the child.

The head must then circulate all the written advice to those who are attending the meeting, inviting additional comments from those asked to attend. The time-scale for these reports is important. Visiting professionals are unlikely to want to write a report without visiting the school to see the child. They will need to fit this into a busy schedule and must be given maximum notice of the dates by which their advice is needed. Parents may need support on submitting their advice and may welcome a pre-review meeting, especially if it is the first annual review after the statement was made or at transition times when their child is due to change school.

An informal meeting may prepare the parent for the much bigger and more formal review meeting. Parents usually find annual reviews stressful, so the preparation meeting can provide an opportunity to answer their questions and ensure they feel confident that their views have been noted. On the day of the meeting, the room should be prepared with sufficient chairs arranged so that parents, their friend and child, if present, can sit together and near a known teacher or other member of staff. The room should be one where there will not be interruptions to interfere with the meeting.

At the review meeting

The head or chairperson introduces themselves and others and makes clear the purpose of the annual review meeting, which is to:

- make sure the parents' views are heard;
- make sure the child's views are heard;
- consider the teacher's reports of progress towards statement targets or those set by the previous annual review;
- consider advice from other professionals, including those not present;
- note any changes in the child's circumstances;
- consider current provision;
- decide on suitable targets for the coming year;
- consider any further actions required and by whom;
- decide whether the statement is appropriate or needs amendment by the LEA;
- decide whether the statement should continue or cease to be maintained.

After the review

The head must prepare the review report which summarises the outcomes of the review meeting and sets targets for the coming year. They then circulate this report to all those concerned with the review. The report must be sent to the LEA by the end of term. The LEA must then review the statement in the light of the report and may:

> Recommend amendments to a statement if:
> 1. Significant new needs have emerged which are not recorded on the statement.
> 2. Significant needs which are recorded on the statement are no longer present.
> 3. The provision should be amended to meet the child's changing needs and the targets specified at the review meeting, or
> 4. The child should change schools, either at the point of transfer between school phases, for example infant to junior or primary to secondary, or
> 5. When a child's needs would more appropriately be met in a different school, for example by inclusion in the mainstream.
>
> (Code of Practice 2001, Chapter 9)

The SEN tribunal

The SEN tribunal was set up by the Education Act 1993. It considers parents' appeals against decisions of the LEA about a child's special educational needs where the parents cannot reach agreement with the LEA. The Code of Practice (2001) states that parents have the right to appeal to the SEN tribunal if:

- They disagree with the LEA's decision not to assess and they, the parents, have been involved in requesting that assessment. (Code of Practice 2001, 7:90)
- After making a statutory assessment, the LEA does not issue a statement but issues a 'note in lieu'. (Code of Practice 2001, 8:15)
- They disagree with the description of the child's needs in Part 2 of the statement (description of special educational provision), and in Part 3 of the statement (the school named, or if no school is named, that fact) or Part 4 of the statement. (Code of Practice 2001, 8:108–8:110)
- The LEA refuses to reassess the child's SEN and the parents' request was made more than six months after any previous assessment. (Code of Practice 2001, 7:97)
- There are named changes of school (e.g. at phase changes). (Code of Practice 2001, 8:132)
- They disagree with the LEA's decision not to maintain a statement. (Code of Practice 2001, 8:120)

Parents *cannot* use the SEN tribunal to complain about the way the LEA is carrying out an assessment, providing help as stated, or the way the school is meeting their child's SEN. Nor can they use the tribunal to appeal against the description of non-educational provision in Parts 5 and 6 of the statement.

In all cases where parents disagree with the LEA decision there must be ample opportunity for discussion with an officer and any relevant professional. The LEA must inform the parents of their right to appeal to the SEN tribunal. The parents should also be given information about parent partnership and disagreement services and informed that their right to appeal cannot be affected by any disagreement resolution procedure (Code of Practice 2001, Chapter 8).

The first appeals to the tribunal began in January 1995 – evidence suggests the number of appeals is increasing each year. Although the intention was not to make them confrontational or to populate them with lawyers, this has often been the case. Parents do not need to be represented by a lawyer, but many have chosen to do so, although legal aid is only available for preparation and not presentation of the case.

The tribunal is now called the Special Educational Needs and Disability Tribunal (SENDIST). The new title reflects responsibility for appeals brought under either special educational needs legislation or the Disability Discrimination Act (1995), as amended by the Special Educational Needs and Disability Act (2001). The tribunal has specific powers. Each tribunal is chaired by a lawyer, drawn from a list appointed by the Lord Chancellor. The tribunal is completed by two lay members, drawn from a list appointed by the Secretary of State. These members will have knowledge and experience of children with special educational needs or, in a disability appeal, expertise in aspects of disability.

The school's role in tribunal cases

School staff, such as the head teacher, SENCO or year head, may be asked to attend as witnesses by either the LEA or the parents. Where a member of staff is reluctant to attend as a witness voluntarily, the individual may be required to attend through an order issued by the tribunal. School staff may be expected to provide detailed information about the child's special educational needs (or disability), the actions taken by the school to meet these identified needs and evidence of the progress made by the pupil. They may also have to respond to questions from the tribunal members, parents or the LEA on issues such as how the school allocates their resources from the SEN budget, how support is organised and how the curriculum is differentiated to match the IEP targets.

It is wise therefore to have an agreed policy, not only for ordinary complaints to the school, but for cases where the parent may appeal against an LEA decision – whether this is a decision not to assess or re-assess a child, not to issue a statement, or about the actual contents of a statement. In preparing its response to the appeal, the LEA may expect the SENCO to help produce detailed evidence in the form of well-kept records, showing both the pupil's progress and the types of intervention and support given by the school. The pupils' and parents' views over time will be an important part of this evidence. Class teachers may sometimes be required to produce evidence of curriculum work of the pupil.

Sometimes schools may agree with the parents' appeal to the tribunal against the LEA. In other situations schools might agree with the LEA. In both cases the school can feel caught between the LEA and the parent, and so the whole context of the tribunal hearing and its preparation can cause stress for all concerned. Where parents have appealed against an LEA decision, there are two very important requirements for the school. Firstly, the paperwork has to be in good order, but must reflect the requirements of the Code of Practice. It is particularly important to be able to demonstrate that IEPs have been in place and reviewed over time; this applies to pupils with statements as much as those at earlier stages. Secondly, everything should have been done to maintain normal professional relationships with the parents, or their 'named person'. Staff need not agree with everything about the parents' appeal or the LEA's response, indeed the school should at all times focus its contribution, supported by evidence upon factual information about the educational needs of the child and the provision necessary to ensure success in learning. School staff should be aware throughout the process of appeal that they have to continue to work closely with the parents after the hearing and that the LEA and parents must comply with the Tribunal Order.

The tribunal process is very stressful and lengthy for parents, and it is not always clear whether it benefits the child to any great extent. Parent partnership schemes have been very effective in offering mediation and consultation to parents who disagree with school or LEA decisions. The Government now expects LEAs to take positive action to try to resolve issues without recourse to the tribunal.

However, this must not deny the parents' rights to appeal if they wish.

Preparing for an Ofsted inspection

The inspection team will be looking at how the school's policy and provision is working and how provision for SEN permeates the school's organisational and curriculum structures and practice. Inspectors will also collect information about the school's results and pupil achievement. They may ask how the assessment policy is cross-referenced to the record-keeping of those with SEN. They may inspect evidence to see that IEPs and annual reviews show current achievement and targets for improvement as well as a means of monitoring progress. They may inquire about how pupils are involved in setting their targets. Inspectors will also look at pupils' behaviour and relationships and may ask if pupils with SEN are free from bullying, whether they attend regularly and are punctual.

Observations of teaching and planning documents should demonstrate that the curricular delivery gives pupils with SEN access and opportunity to take part in a full, balanced and relevant curriculum. Questions will be asked about whether schemes of work reflect the differing rates and styles of learning and whether learning support is adequate in extent and nature. Questions will also be asked about whether alternative therapies and programmes are built into the curriculum effectively.

Preparation by the SENCO for an Ofsted inspection

The SENCO is likely to be given some time to meet inspectors and should have the following documents and information to hand:

- the SEN records showing information about the number of pupils on *School Action* and *School Action Plus* as well as those with statements.
- up to date IEPs and annual reviews showing targets set, review dates and deployment of resources.
- the SEN policy, giving information about the school as listed in Schedule 1 (see Appendix 2b). This is to include evidence of how this is monitored and evaluated annually.
- staffing information: qualifications and job descriptions for SENCO and support staff.
- the SENCO's timetable and those of support staff, showing how support is deployed, monitored and evaluated.
- school prospectus and other communications with parents, such as standard letters. (The SENCO is only a part of the learning support system and others may be responsible for support management.)
- systems of passing information to and from staff should be clearly explained. This should include ways IEPs are reviewed and how parents' and pupils' views are incorporated.
- information about staff development opportunities for all staff, including induction for new staff.
- links with other schools or colleges, including how records and information are passed on to the receiving school.
- information about the use of outside agencies and services and how liaison is timed.
- targets and action points from previous inspections and the school's SEN annual policy statements to parents.
- information about the SEN budget. SENCOs should know their own department's budget and be able to discuss the school's priorities for resourcing SEN.

Knowing about the SEN budget

As discussed in Chapter 2, the head and governors continue to hold overall responsibility for determining the policy and approach to SEN and for setting up appropriate funding and staffing arrangements. The governors' annual report must inform parents about the success of the SEN policy and any significant changes and the allocation of resources over the previous year to pupils with SEN. It is not the SENCO's role to determine budgets or policies, but it will be useful if their advice is sought by governors and if, in turn, the SENCO understands the main principles which the governors apply in deciding how resources will be allocated between and amongst pupils with SEN.

Many SENCOs report that gaining access to budget and resource information is difficult. The funds which are devolved from the LEA to the school under the LMS schemes are known and in the public domain. Some of these are worked out by the number and age of pupils on roll (APWU), others by the funding allocated for additional needs (ANS). These may be allocated by the LEA using a proxy indicator of those eligible to free school meals or other indices decided by the LEA such as those on the SEN register or mobility of pupils. But how these funds are used is decided by the governing body.

Monitoring and reviewing the school's SEN policy

As discussed in more detail in Chapter 2, there is an expectation within the requirements for SEN policies as listed in the Code of Practice and expanded on in Circular 6/94, that every school will review their SEN policy annually. In practice, schools have often left this task until an Ofsted inspection is due.

Unfortunately, it also seems that many schools have not set targets or success criteria, so a new SENCO may have to do this for the first time when wishing to set up a review cycle. It is important to recognise that a review may cover all aspects of policy in a general manner and then focus on one or two areas in greater depth.

These priority areas may arise from external inspections or from staff in school identifying some aspect that needs improvement or has not previously been covered. (Activities 2 and 6 may help this process.)

Summary

This chapter has described the core of the SENCO's administrative work which is:

- the maintenance of paperwork and organisation of review procedures associated with the Code of Practice;
- the monitoring of IEPs and associated curriculum planning and assessment for all pupils with SEN;
- preparation of paperwork or information to feed into reviews of the school policy or development plan, or for an Ofsted inspection.

The prime aim of all of these tasks is to improve the opportunities for pupils with SEN to learn effectively, access the curriculum, make progress and be valued and full members of the school community. The SENCO can help make this happen if they can both organise efficiently and work in a supportive way with all concerned. This consultative role will be considered in the next chapter.

CHAPTER 10

Working with People: the Consultative Role

The role of SENCO requires an ability to work with colleagues, pupils and parents, as well as other professionals. Much of this work is of a consultative nature. Everyone looks to the SENCO for support, advice and even counselling. How much of this rather less formal work any particular SENCO can do, depends on a number of factors. The first of these factors is the SENCO's own feeling of confidence. This will be stronger when based on a feeling of competence built up through knowledge and skills gained from experience and training. It takes time to acquire this confidence and competence so as to be in a position to support others and act as a change agent in a school. There are a number of courses running nationally and locally designed to cover the National Standards for SENCOs. There are also often local support groups run by the LEA for SENCOs.

The second of the factors which will enhance and facilitate the consultative role, is the school's general policies and ethos. It will matter how, for example, parents are perceived as part of the school community:

● Is there an honest, open attitude towards partnership with parents?
● Are parents' views welcomed and considered when policies are being developed?
● Are pupils' perspectives valued in the way policies and procedures for the whole population in the school have been developed?
● Are staff valued and given praise by senior management?

The needs of teachers have to be met if they in turn are to meet the needs of children, especially those children who are more difficult to teach.

Galloway (1985) defined children with special needs as those children that caused teachers stress, either because they couldn't learn and make progress as expected, or because they could not conform to the norms of behaviour expected by the teacher.

If the school is set up to support staff and provide them with ways of dealing with stressful situations collaboratively, the role of the SENCO will be a more effective part of this process. Where the school is not as supportive to teachers, pupils or parents as it should be, the consultative role for the SENCO will be much harder. He or she will have to choose those parts of the 'system' which can be worked with to achieve some success. The consultative role will have to begin with small actions wherever possible. This is in order to preserve the SENCO's own health and ability to cope with what is already a very complex job.

It is better to find one colleague who can be positively supported and helped to gain confidence and competence, than to try to do too much too fast. Don't expect too much change to occur too quickly.

Where the system is more developed and there are already many positive features, such as many colleagues who have gained competence in meeting individual needs, working with parents and working collaboratively with others, then the scale of what can be achieved will be greater and the rate of change faster.

The National Standards for SENCOs (TTA 1998) lists the skills needed by SENCOs. These include the ability to:

- create and foster commitment and confidence among staff to meet the needs of pupils with SEN;
- negotiate and consult parents and external agencies;
- explain to pupils the objectives of any interventions.

This chapter looks at these aspects of the SENCO's consultative role:

- working with pupils: considering pupil perspectives and rights;
- working in partnership with parents: dealing with stress and complaints;
- working with colleagues: giving support and training.

Each section will look both at the personal skills of the SENCO and features of the whole-school approach, which together contribute to effective development of the consultative role.

Enhancing pupil perspectives

To achieve an understanding of the pupil's own view of their school experience and their educational needs requires an ability on the behalf of the teacher to change perspective. Teachers have to let go of their position of authority, for a short time, and view the world of the classroom from the pupil's point of view. This may best be done through becoming a careful observer for certain times and taking detailed notes. If someone else can manage the class for a short session while this observation takes place, it may be easier to be free to observe.

Learning to be a skilled observer

Learning observation skills gives teachers a useful tool for assessment and general problem-solving. Observation can be for set times (e.g. ten minutes) or of specific events or of a specific context, such as the playground. Starting the observation without a precise focus may be possible, but increasingly focusing on an intended feature may give more insight. If pupil perspectives are the focus, this may need to be combined with interview techniques. There are a number of observation techniques given in Appendix 10a.

Accurate observation for as little as ten minutes, if focused and prepared, can give insights into a particular area of concern, whether an individual pupil or a group. Always remember that observation will be affected by bias, so if more than one adult can observe to a prepared schedule the results may be more reliable.

Using other techniques

Another way to get a pupil's perspective is, of course, to ask the pupil to talk about or express their views. This can be by direct questions about an aspect of their work such as reading or homework, or it can be by more open-ended questioning about school or friends. Open-ended interviewing is difficult for some teachers to do, partly because of time constraints, partly because it is a skill to be learnt. Sometimes other adults, ancillary helpers or support professionals may fare better because they may offer less threat to pupils or have time to see pupils in a more relaxed environment.

The whole class can be given exercises to evaluate an aspect of their own learning, possibly to give ratings about how confident they feel about various aspects of their learning. For younger pupils, faces with different expressions can be used to rate answers instead of words (see Appendix 10b).

It is more difficult to gain a view of pupil perspective where the pupil lacks the language to express their thoughts and feelings in words. In these cases observations from more than one adult may need to be combined to give a feel for the pupil's perspective. Ancillary helpers' and parents' observations about different aspects of the pupil's development and feelings of self-worth are very helpful in putting together a joint perspective. The use of video cameras and tape recorders can help collect valuable data in cases where more direct questioning is difficult – for example, the developmentally young, or pupils with language impairment. These would not be kept as a long-term record, but might help analyse complex observations.

Drawings and symbolic representations of situations as perceived during play can all add to the teacher's understanding of pupil perspectives.

The above approaches take time for just one child, and cannot be used for all the pupils in a class or on the SEN register. Different methods can be selected for different children and at different times. It is useful however if, as part of training sessions, teachers can practise some of the skills required in collecting and collating information which will enhance their ability to look at pupil perspectives. For some teachers, the exercise of *really* trying to understand one pupil, from a child's point of view, is a revelation (see Appendix 10a and b).

School policy taking pupil perspectives into account

The Code of Practice (2001), Chapter 3, discusses pupil participation in some detail. Other guidance can be found in the *SEN Toolkit* (Section 4). Children and young people have the right to be involved in making decisions and exercising choices. They have a unique knowledge of their needs and their views should be listened to and taken into account.

It will help if the school develops procedures for regularly taking note of pupil perspectives. For example, IEP proformas need to have space to note the pupils' views (see Appendix 3a). Regular conferencing times when the pupils' views are taken down can be built into the review procedure for IEPs or given to all pupils. The records of achievement approach to recording progress, as part of the school's assessment policy, will enhance the work of those dealing with special needs. As part of the review of the SEN policy, the following questions need to be asked:

- Do we take account of pupil viewpoints and perspectives?
- Do we have procedures and times when we can note pupil viewpoints and perspectives?
- Do pupil views and perspectives influence policy-making in the school?

Opinions will of course vary amongst staff as to whether pupils' views should be given any priority. Some staff may even fundamentally disagree with the principle of listening to pupils. In such situations the golden rules of 'small is beautiful' and 'working with the positive parts of the system' will need to be kept in mind. SENCOs need to keep the pupil perspective in mind when planning for individuals with SEN. It is worth considering the focus on childrens' rights in the 1989 Children Act, but despite this, children seem to have far fewer rights in schools than in relation to health and social services. It could seem that the whole issue of the rights of children is subordinated to the rights of parents and of the educational establishments.

Working in partnership with parents

Just as understanding the pupils' viewpoints needs a change of perspective for the teacher, so often does understanding the parents' viewpoints. If a true partnership with parents is to be established, then the teacher or the SENCO needs to learn to listen to and value the parents' expertise about their own child or their concerns about his or her progress.

To do this effectively, it is necessary to learn new skills. Teachers are good at expressing themselves and activating ideas. They may not be quite as good as listeners. Listening effectively in the consultative role is a skill to be learnt and practised.

Emphatic listening

In this mode the listener obeys certain ground rules. These are:

- keep eye contact;
- keep still, do not distract your listener by fiddling with pens, etc.;
- keep your own comments to a minimum, such as 'I see', 'right', 'I understand' and 'yes';
- if longer comments are required, make these reflective, i.e. feed back the main point as you understood it, so it can be checked; use these comments to summarise points and check that you have understood what was said.
- don't be afraid to feed back feelings as well as facts: 'That must have made you angry', 'You were upset by. . .'.

Such listening sessions will need time limits, which should be set in advance if possible: 'We've got half an hour, please tell me your concerns, worries . . . and we will try to find some answers to the problems.' Check that the parent is happy for you to take notes. Often it is not a good idea to do this if you are really trying to listen. You cannot keep eye contact and write notes. It may be a good idea to make time to summarise at the end of the session and agree a few points which can be written down. Establishing a feeling of trust is more important than note-taking at this point. Once the problem has been identified and the parent feels they were listened to, it is possible to move into a *problem-solving* mode.

Problem-solving

As a first step, this requires that the problem has been clearly identified. Next, actions can be jointly planned with the parent to try to solve the problem. Problem-solving again needs a sensitive approach from the teacher, while setting boundaries for what is achievable in school within limited resources. Wherever possible, the parents will feel more of a partner if they can suggest ideas to be discussed, perhaps offering to help in some way at home or in school. Joint targets can then be set and a date to review progress made. Copies of written notes of meetings should be given to parents wherever possible.

Parents' rights and involvement

Parents are defined under the Children Act 1989 as those who have parental responsibility for the child or who have care of the child (full description in Appendix 10c). Over the last two decades, legislation has increased parents' rights in relation to schools, choices and information, as is shown in the summary of Education Acts given below.

Summary of Education Acts in relation to parents' rights

Education Acts since 1980 have given rights to all parents. The 1981 and 1993 Acts gave rights to parents of pupils with SEN.

1980 Education Act

In this legislation, parents, other than those whose child had a statement, were granted the right to choose the school they wished to send their children to. Parents were also given the right to be represented on the governing bodies of schools.

1981 Education Act

Parents' involvement in the formal assessment of their child increased under this Act. Parents also were given the right to appeal first to the LEA and then to the Secretary of State about decisions made by the LEA as a result of making a multi-professional assessment for a statement.

1986 Education Acts

The first of two Education Acts passed in 1986 required increased parental representation on the governing bodies of schools. Governors were required to present an annual report to parents and to have a meeting with parents at the school in order to discuss the report.

1988 Education Act

This Act granted parents the right to send their children to any school of their choice so long as it had room for them. It also required that parents are sent an annual report on their children's progress and it gave schools the opportunity of opting out of LEA control if a majority of parents voted in favour of this.

1992 Education Act

It was this Act that set out the new inspection procedures for schools. Teams of independent inspectors coordinated by the Office for Standards in Education (Ofsted) were to inspect all maintained schools. Parents had a right to meet the inspectors before the inspection to discuss any issue they wished which could include how the needs of pupils with SEN were met and how parents were involved in reviews.

1996 Education Act (incorporating the Education Act 1993)

These Acts made changes to emphasise parental rights. The SEN tribunal gave the parents rights of appeal against LEA decisions related to final assessment (see Chapter 9 for more detail). The Code of Practice (2001) Chapter 2 emphasises the importance of working with parents.

The SEN and Disability Discrimination Act (2002)

This Act extended the right for parents to use the Tribunal for claims against unlawful discrimination in schools for those with disabilities.

Partnership with parents: Schedule 1:15

The school's policy should contain a clear statement of the arrangements for ensuring close working partnerships with parents of children with special educational needs. This will mean incorporating parents' views in assessment and reviews and ensuring parents are fully informed about the school's procedures and are made welcome in the school.

Much of this will be achieved if a policy for parents of all pupils is inclusive and enhances participation. SEN policy should not be an add-on, but an integral part of the school's general way of working with parents. Mallett (1995) suggests that the following might be ways of doing this:

- explaining the graduated response to meeting SEN, at a parents' meeting;
- holding a 'hands-on' differentiation workshop, so that parents, teachers and classroom assistants can share making the curriculum accessible;
- involving parents in the monitoring and evaluating of the school's performance relating to the targets set for the SEN policy.

Developing partnerships

If schools have listened to parents when developing other policies, then parents' perspectives will already be reflected. Parents of pupils with SEN are however particularly vulnerable. Parents of children with difficulties and disabilities may lack confidence themselves, may even feel guilty (unjustifiably) about their child. Such parents are not always confident enough to ask for these views to be taken into account, or even know their rights. It is therefore essential that the SENCO gives parents information about these rights to be listened to. Parents need to have the five-staged assessment procedure explained. They need to know about LEA services which may be called on to support their child. School provision for SEN also needs to be explained.

There are a few parents however who seem to have all too much confidence and knowledge of their rights. Such parents can pose a threat to some teachers and the SENCO in particular. To make a partnership with these parents requires skills of assertiveness and the ability to set limits, in particular:

- knowing how to say 'no';
- knowing how to limit time spent.

Such parents can be aggressive, even rude. Their feelings of anger, guilt and frustration over finding their child is not making expected progress can be let loose on an unsuspecting and caring SENCO, with the result that instead of a partnership, a confrontation occurs. As Dale (1996) explains, parents can go through a 'psychic shock' when they first hear of their child's disability. The first phase may only last a day or so, at which time they need sympathy and understanding. After that their need is for information to help them orientate better. The next step will be to use a problem-solving approach to help parents come to terms with the new situation. This situation is of course best avoided by preventative strategies. Emphatic listening can still help establish a rapport followed by a structured problem-solving session. If the parents feel they really have been listened to and their viewpoints taken into account, they may be able to calm down and look for joint practical solutions.

If, however, their feelings seem irrational and solutions are beyond the resources of the school, it may be necessary to seek help either from other members of the school, the head for example, or outside professionals.

Almost all parents can be brought into a partnership situation. Difficulties arise when promises are broken, resources lent do not come back to school or the pupil is absent intermittently or for long periods. In many of these cases the teacher's motivation to work in partnership with parents dwindles. The parents' own needs can only be addressed by the teacher, as far as they affect the pupil. Parents' own adult needs cannot be addressed by the school, although it is possible sometimes to get a personal referral for help.

The questions SENCOs need to keep in mind when working with parents are:

- What is a possible outcome of this meeting which will benefit the child?
- What resources are available from the school, or the community, to support this child and parent?

● What is achievable in the immediate future, and in the more distant future?

Being able to summarise the answers to these questions and feed back to the parents in a positive manner will be a way of recording the meeting.

Dealing with complaints

Schedule 1 (Regulation 2(I), 1:12) states that the school SEN policy must include a section on how complaints will be dealt with:

> The policy should make clear to parents and children with SEN how they can make a complaint about the provision made for their child at the school and how that complaint will be dealt with by the school.

Schools usually have a general complaints system, but will need to give particular attention to SEN complaints. Often it is to the class teacher or the SENCO that the parent first turns. If the matter can be dealt with easily and quietly, this is best. It should be kept clearly in mind that the head teacher has the final responsibility for the school along with the governors. It is important therefore that procedures are clearly set out and published and not left to chance. If schools make sure parents are fully informed throughout the assessment procedures and given access to the LEA Parent Partnership Scheme as early as possible, it should be possible to allay fears and avoid complaints. The *SEN Toolkit* (Section 2) gives further information about Parent Partnership services.

Supporting colleagues

Much of what has been said in the previous sections applies to working successfully with colleagues. They too need someone to share concerns, so listening skills will apply here as will problem-solving strategies. Often colleagues only need to be reassured that they are doing the right thing. Being able to describe their problem, express their concerns and anxieties may be sufficient to produce the feeling of being supported. It may be wise to follow this up by observation of the child or group in question. Fuller assessment may be part of the solution. An interview with pupil and parents may be indicated.

It is not the SENCO's role to know all answers to all questions. What they can do is to facilitate the *problem-solving abilities* of their colleagues and help them find solutions which they feel will work. These solutions may require the SENCO to work collaboratively with the class or child, or they may be to request precise advice on strategies concerning resources. Being able to enter into productive dialogues with colleagues is *the skill* the SENCO will need to develop most. It is, of course, more likely that the SENCO will also have knowledge of a particular strategy or resource to help a particular child, if they have experience of a wide range of SEN themselves or have access to specialist advice.

The SENCO's role in supporting in-service training for SEN

The TTA Standards document states that one of the SENCO's roles in leading and managing staff is to advise on, contribute to, or coordinate the professional development of staff to increase their response to pupils with SEN and to provide support and training of newly qualified teachers.

Robertson (1999) suggests the SENCO may be the member of staff best suited to induct newly qualified teachers in the ways to include pupils with SEN in their classes. The training of new teachers should have covered aspects of SEN work but this varies from college to college, so some new teachers may need a lot of information and time.

It is often seen as central to the SENCO's role to take the lead during in-service sessions on the various aspects of SEN. Just how feasible this is again depends on the existing knowledge and competence level of the SENCOs themselves. Many aspects of SEN policy and procedures can be dealt with in-house by the SENCO. It needs to be recognised, however, that the more specialist areas may not be known by anyone in one school and it is then that help needs to be brought in from outside services or professionals. SENCOs may also wish to set up information corners in the staff room and provide all staff with a folder. This could include guidance on how the graduated response will be operated in the school and how contacts to outside agencies can be made.

CHAPTER 11

Working Together towards Inclusive Practice

The *Programme for Action* (DfEE 1998c) stated that the government will promote further inclusion within mainstream schools where parents want it and appropriate support can be provided.

The document admits that the challenge this produces for schools should not be underestimated and that solutions should be pragmatic and put the needs of individual children first. It continues by saying: 'Inclusion is a process not a fixed state. It should mean the participation of all pupils in learning which leads to the highest possible achievement and the participation of young people in the full range of social experiences and opportunities once they have left school.'

Florian (1998) agrees that there is a gap between policy and implementation which must be addressed. She says that 'if inclusion is the opportunity for persons with a disability to participate fully in all activities that typify everyday society, this transcends the concept of normalisation'. This is an important idea, because it means changing attitudes so that those with disabilities are not treated as a minority group, labelled and given special treatment. It means *including* activities for everyone which previously might have been seen as 'only for a disabled group'. An example of this might be for all pupils in a school learning to sign rather than only those who are deaf (McKeown 2000).

This means considering the conditions needed for inclusion. As Florian (1998) suggests, these might include:

- opportunities for pupil participation in decision-making;
- positive attitudes about the learning abilities of all pupils;
- teacher knowledge of a range of difficulties and ways to overcome barriers to learning.

Disability rights and inclusive education

Rieser (1995), writing from the viewpoint of the Disabled People's movement, proposes that SEN should be part of an equal opportunities policy and not treated as a separate issue. He points out that 'the focus on the individual child rather than the whole curriculum and how it needs to change, has led to isolation, exclusion, separation, and sometimes compulsory segregation' (p. 40).

He explains that the medical model, which typifies so much SEN work, results in seeing the disabled person as having a problem which needs treatment. (The term disabled is here interpreted as including all those with impairments or chronic illnesses, as well as those with any learning or emotional or behavioural difficulty.) The social model, on the other hand, recognises that disabled people may have a wide range of impairments with varying loss of function, but proposes that it is the limitations of opportunities which creates disability. This is due to physical, social or attitudinal barriers.

Adopting a social model of SEN within a whole-school approach will mean thinking of ways to break down such barriers. Some of this will mean returning to policies against bullying, for example, and addressing name-calling using negative descriptions of body and mind; or reviewing the behaviour policy to include the inculcation of attitudes of mutual respect and strong equality principles. Any successful policy which allows pupils to express their thoughts and feelings with confidence in a climate of trust will benefit everyone. Disability equality training opportunities for teachers, governors, parents and pupils will be required to achieve this.

The *Index for Inclusion* (Booth et al.) is aimed at helping schools develop inclusive practice. It is a self review audit to produce policies and evolve practices within a culture where everyone is valued. It begins with the suggestion that a co-ordinating team is set up by the school which may include a 'critical friend' from outside the school. This group then examines indicators and questions about inclusive practice and notes the school's stage of development and then sets up policies for moving the school forward. The index attempts to move away from the label of special educational need for both the coordination and the policy, preferring titles like inclusion coordinator or inclusion policy. This index is now available in all primary and secondary schools and may help the senior management team when considering the issue of inclusion.

Circular 0774/2001 gives guidance to schools, LEAs and health and social services on the practical operation for inclusion. This circular states that schools and others should actively seek to remove the barriers to learning and participation that can hinder or exclude pupils with SEN. It makes reference to the National Curriculum 2000 Inclusion Statement (see Chapter 4).

The SEN Disability Act (2001) strengthens the right to mainstream education and gives enforceable civil rights to disabled pupils and students. This relates to admission, provision and exclusion. The definition of who could be considered disabled is spelt out in the DRC Code of Practice (2002).

Planning duties

The Disability Discrimination Act (1995) (Sections 28 D and E) sets out the planning duties that schools will need to develop in order to avoid unlawful discrimination against disabled pupils. This means that schools and LEAs have a planning duty to:

- increase physical accessibility (this covers anything relating to building design, lighting and signing, fixtures and fittings, and furnishings);
- improve access to the curriculum for disabled pupils, for example teaching and learning arrangements, deployment of staff, timetabling, and staff training;
- improve provision of information, such as hand-outs, text books, and information about school trips. This might be provided in Braille, large print, through sign language or on audio tape.

Draft accessibility plans are to be in place by April 2003. The purpose of these plans is to be anticipatory, to gradually prepare schools for disabled pupils who may be admitted in the future. Although SENCOs have no direct responsibility for planning, they may be asked to contribute to working parties, especially in areas related to curriculum access. Further advice on accessible planning is available in Circular LEA/0168 (2002).

The SENCO's role as change agent

One role the SENCO may find themselves holding will be that of a 'change agent' within the school as an organisation. Working towards more inclusive practice is a process which will be ongoing. If it is to be effective, other teachers will need to be involved and senior management will need to give their support.

The purpose of this final chapter is to examine the SENCO's role in its totality within the context of whole-school development. Schools are being challenged to become more effective by setting targets for improvement against national and local benchmarks. The SENCO will have an important part to play in a school's development by keeping the quality of teaching and learning for *all* pupils on the agenda. How does the child with special educational needs fare in this search for school improvement? Are they to be welcomed as part of a diverse community and valued for their contribution and achievements; or will the focus on publishing results and ever improving standards make schools afraid to include these pupils on their roll?

One characteristic of a good school is that it has established good management of resources which maximise the potential effectiveness of the whole institution. Resources of time, people and equipment will be required to meet the identified range of pupils with special needs. Policies will require strategic planning by those in management to include the careful monitoring of these resources. This policy and resource allocation must be clearly understood by everyone, including parents.

However, a successful inclusion policy is as much to do with attitudes and values as resources. Developing effective inclusive education remains a challenge to most schools, even when it is a part of their mission. *'Society is made up of other people's children'*, was a remark frequently made by Joan Sallis when talking to teachers. By this she meant that we cannot afford to educate only the high achievers or the easy-to-teach children, because every child will be part of our future.

The SENCO should always consider the individual needs of pupils who attend the school. One of the important ways that inclusive practice will move forward is if teachers listen to pupil and parent perspectives and are prepared to adopt flexible practices which take on board the individual differences. Staff may require help in understanding how they can reduce barriers for pupils with disabilities which may arise from their lack of knowledge of pupil perspectives. Often simple changes in classroom practices will help a broad range of pupils take a fuller part in the school curriculum and in school life.

Inclusion does not end with placement. For a pupil to feel included they should be able to take part socially and have friends. It will be very important for SENCOs to listen to pupils' perspectives on their social well-being as well as monitoring academic progress. For example, pupils with disabilities may find making friends more difficult if they spend too much of their day with LSAs. The peer group may tolerate the pupil with a disability but not know how to fully include them in conversations or games. It may well be that part of a SENCO's role is to ensure that teachers and the peer group have training in disability issues so that ignorance does not produce attitudes which make real inclusion impossible.

Special educational needs as a construct

Everyone builds up their own construct of special needs from their experience and knowledge, both personal and professional. My own research (Cowne 1993) demonstrated how this construct developed for course members as a result of attending courses and working on school-based action research projects. SENCOs and special needs teachers build up their confidence and competence by learning both the theory and practice of individual assessment and teaching, curriculum planning and differentiation, effective classroom management techniques and consultancy skills. Their constructs grew in complexity as the teacher gained more experience and reflected on their own learning. The construct was not fixed, although each individual had a core which was personal to them. It follows that the SENCO's role will also be built up from an interaction between his or her constructs and those of significant numbers of the school's staff. Each school will build its value systems, out of which all the policies, priorities and roles will develop.

But it is only when SENCOs are supported by heads and by what one head called 'a critical number' of other staff, that change in the institution can occur. Head teachers' constructs of SEN are often different from their SENCOs'. Heads think about resource issues, or where advice can be found or how staff development can occur. They often see SEN policy as helping to develop good classroom management and well-planned curriculum differentiation resulting in better standards of teaching in their schools. SEN development therefore becomes a lever for other school development.

O'Hanlon (1993) comments that special needs work is often carried out in 'occupied territory' and the role requires 'barter, negotiation and compromise'. It is complex and emotive, but she argues that conflict is the very centre of institutional change and can be resolved as long as communication is maintained. Her view is of a change agent who works as a reflective practitioner to address these change issues and help resolve the tensions. This confirms my own findings that by engaging in reflective conversations, the SENCO can act as an agent of change. SENCOs on training courses are often asked to develop an area of policy and practice for their course work. This opens up opportunities for change management. My second book, *Developing Inclusive Practice: The SENCO's Role in Managing Change* (2003), gives many practical examples of how SENCOs on training courses have developed areas of school policy and practice.

Time management and the SENCO role

Reviewing policy will include considering which tasks are to be performed by the SENCO along with other roles and responsibilities (see Chapter 2). The inclusion of a wider range of pupils has resulted in more support personnel to manage (see Chapters 6 and 7). There is an ever increasing need to develop an inclusive way of delivering the curriculum (see Chapters 4 and 5).

Tensions exist between wishing to use time to support pupils, parents and colleagues (the consultative role) and dealing with ever increasing paperwork (the coordinating role) (see Chapters 8, 9 and 10). The most significant dilemma is between using the IEP for individualising support in contrast to diversifying resources to support a differentiated curriculum for all (see Chapters 3 and 4).

The publishing of the TTA Standards has meant that the role of the SENCO is better defined and the status of special needs work enhanced. Time management remains one of the most important issues identified by SENCOs, one which can make or mar their effectiveness. The Code of Practice (2001) suggests governing bodies and head teachers should give careful thought to the SENCO's timetable in the context of the resources available to the school. The Code also suggests that administrative staff time be allocated to help SENCOs, particularly those in secondary schools, but individual schools will make their own judgements and choices about allocating resources and therefore time to SENCOs, so they can perform their role effectively.

The scope of this book

This book has attempted to give practical advice, theoretical background and ideas to support SEN policy development and the SENCO's role within that development. Some readers will be experienced and for them I hope to have stimulated thought and challenged them to further reading. Others will have been more recently appointed and will need some of the detail the book provides. However, this book does not have all the answers. Some questions require local knowledge, some further research. The Code of Practice (2001) will need careful examining, as will the new Code of Practice for schools (2002) related to the Disability Discrimination Act and the circular on Inclusive Schooling DfES 0774 (2001). SENCOs will have a significant role to play as long as they remain reflective practitioners, able to manage change in themselves, and hold meaningful conversations with colleagues and parents to develop the expertise and attitudes to make ordinary schools special places for all pupils.

Whole-school Policy for
Special Educational Needs

Activity 1: Roles and Responsibilities for SEN

Choose either the primary or secondary sheet on the following pages.

Step 1. The first column of the grid lists tasks which are normally seen as essential in relation to the maintenance and management of your whole-school policy. Refer to TTA 1998 – *National Standards for Special Educational Needs Co-ordinators.* Change these tasks to suit your own school if you wish.

Step 2. The first row lists people who will be involved in these tasks in either primary or secondary schools. Change the 'people' to suit your own school if you wish.

Step 3. Now decide at what level each person has responsibility for each of the tasks. Write one of the letters below in each box.

A = Action Level; S = Strategic Level; I = Need for Information Level

Step 4. Draw up an action plan in relation to roles and responsibilities. Check:

- Is anyone's role going to change significantly?
- How will all staff be informed of changes?
- How much time will be needed for individuals with Action roles?
- How will this be achieved – do governors need information?
- How will information flow between A, S and I roles?

Step 5. Discuss evaluation criteria and timing:

- When will this plan be monitored and evaluated?
- Who will be asked for their views?

Set review date and write the main action points into your development plan.

Activity 1: Primary – Analysis of SEN coordination roles and responsibilities

People / Tasks	Class Teacher	SENCO and/or Support Staff	Year Coordinator	Head Teacher	Governor(s)
Identify and assess pupils with SEN					
Maintain SEN register					
Write IEPs					
Differentiate curriculum					
Give advice on curriculum materials					
Monitor pupil progress					
Organise review procedures for IEPs and statements					
Manage support staff					
Liaise with outside agencies					
Liaise/work with parents					
Provide in-service SEN training					
Inform governors of changes in policy and resource implications					

© Elizabeth Cowne, 2003

Activity 1: Secondary – Analysis of SEN coordination roles and responsibilities

Tasks \ People	Subject Teacher	Form Teacher	SENCO/ Support Staff	Head of Year	Head of Dept.	SMT	Governor(s)
Identify and assess pupils with SEN							
Maintain SEN records							
Write IEPs							
Differentiate curriculum							
Give advice on resourcing curriculum materials							
Monitor pupil progress							
Organise review procedures for IEPs and statements							
Manage support staff							
Deliver in-service SEN training							
Liaise with outside agencies							
Liaise/work with parents							
Inform governors of changes in policy and resource implications							

Activity 2: Audit of Whole-school Policy
Reviewing your Whole-school Policy for Special Educational Needs

The following exercise covers most aspects of a whole-school SEN policy. Select those that are most appropriate to your school. The aim is to give an opportunity for staff to discuss and reflect on what should be in the school's policy and how it is working at present. Areas for development and differing opinions may be revealed. These can be further explored in a discussion group.

If using this as a staff development exercise, individuals should work in small groups, such as year or curriculum teams, to reach some consensus of opinion on the most important priorities for the next year's work on the policy. This group activity starts by collating the group's individual results and looking for the biggest/smallest gap between the upper and lower line of markings.

Alternatively this audit could be given to staff as a questionnaire. The analysis of the data will provide information to the SENCO or the steering group.

Activity 2: Instructions

This checklist contains 15 statements about SEN policy or arrangements in schools. Its purpose is to help identify those points of your school's policy or arrangements in which there is scope for improvement. Each statement is followed by two lines – a) and b), for rating on a 1–5 scale.

Line a)   Ring the number which represents the extent to which this **ought** to be in the whole-school policy on SEN.
1 = *must not be in*; 5 = *must be in*

Line b)   Ring the number which represents your view of the **actual** situation at present.
1 = *not happening at all*; 5 = *happening completely*

If you wish, add two more statements to cover any aspects not already mentioned. Rank these in the same way as the others. The difference between the ratings of the two lines may indicate the school's most important areas for action on policy development. Discussion following this exercise within a staff or in-service meeting will serve as a way to reach consensus over priorities for the next year.

1.   There is an operational policy for SEN which has principles consistent with the Code of Practice (2001).

a) 1   2   3   4   5

b) 1   2   3   4   5

2.   The key principles of the school's SEN policy are known to all staff.

a) 1   2   3   4   5

b) 1   2   3   4   5

3.   There are descriptive guidelines of the roles and responsibilities of staff in relation to SEN. These include roles for governors, head, SENCOs, teachers and TAs.

a) 1   2   3   4   5

b) 1   2   3   4   5

4.   All teaching staff are aware of the procedures used to identify, assess and record the needs of pupils with SEN.

a) 1   2   3   4   5

b) 1   2   3   4   5

5.   There are arrangements in place to organise regular reviews of progress for all pupils with SEN.

a) 1   2   3   4   5

b) 1   2   3   4   5

6.   Pupils are involved in decision-making during planning of their IEPs.

a) 1   2   3   4   5

b) 1   2   3   4   5

7. Staff are supported in the development of a range of teaching strategies, learning activities and support materials which enhance access to the curriculum for pupils with SEN.

   a) 1   2   3   4   5

   b) 1   2   3   4   5

8. Individual planning for pupils with SEN is an integral part of general curriculum planning.

   a) 1   2   3   4   5

   b) 1   2   3   4   5

9. There is a staff development policy for SEN which relates to the school improvement plan and reflects individual staff priorities and needs.

   a) 1   2   3   4   5

   b) 1   2   3   4   5

10. Parents are kept informed of their child's additional needs and are involved in the planning of future targets for their child.

    a) 1   2   3   4   5

    b) 1   2   3   4   5

11. Parents are given information about the school's policy and procedures for SEN.

    a) 1   2   3   4   5

    b) 1   2   3   4   5

12. Support staff have clear roles and are encouraged to work as members of a team to enhance inclusive practice.

    a) 1   2   3   4   5

    b) 1   2   3   4   5

13. Liaison time is available for class or subject teachers to plan effective use of support time.

    a) 1   2   3   4   5

    b) 1   2   3   4   5

14. The school's allocation of resources for SEN is clearly described and understood by the SENCO or other relevant staff.

    a) 1   2   3   4   5

    b) 1   2   3   4   5

15. There are clear procedures known to relevant staff for making referrals to outside agencies.

    a) 1   2   3   4   5

    b) 1   2   3   4   5

Activity 3: Lesson Planning for Differentiation

1. Choose a topic within your subject.

2. Answer questions 1 and 2.

3. Define core objectives for the lesson.
    What should the pupils learn? (Give range of outcomes if necessary.)

4. What different assessment modalities (such as oral, written, demonstration) will be used?

5. Write down prerequisite baseline skills or concepts that you are assuming to present in the class, before you start. (Change boxes to suit yourself.)

6. Think of up to three pupils with IEPs or statements. List the barriers to learning that this topic might produce for these children.

7. Decide if any modifications to your planning are necessary in the light of this discussion.

8. Add extension ideas for your more able pupils or the whole class.

9. If staff development time allows, discuss continuity and cross-curricular issues. What should have been covered by previous lessons or in other subjects? Will this cause confusion to students? Are there 'bridging' needs to cross-refer between subjects?

Activity Pack

Activity 3: Differentiation exercise for Key Stage 1 and 2 lessons

Question 1

Is this realistic to do in the time allocated?

Question 2

Is this relevant to this group of students?

Topic		Extension
	Core curriculum objectives	
Strategies/methods/resources		
	How will outcomes be assessed?	
Modification		

Prerequisite baseline skills

Language (oral)	Language (written)	Social	Key concepts needed
Manipulative	Number	Organisational	

Activity 3: Differentiation exercise for Key Stage 3 lesson

Question 1
Is this realistic to do in the time allocated?

Question 2
Is this relevant to this group of students?

Topic	Extension
Core curriculum objectives e.g. tasks, skills, concepts	
Delivery methods/resources/support	
How will outcomes be assessed?	
Modification	

Social	Subject specific
Thinking	**Organisational**
Linguistic	**Other**
Numerical	

© Elizabeth Cowne, 2003

Activity 4: Provision Mapping Exercise

The following forms could be completed by participants in a training group of SENCOs (or others). List ways in which support is currently being used in each year group, or extract and collate the provision information from the IEPs and statements. Below is a list of potential examples which support staff might be engaged in. You may want to add other activities applicable to your school.

Primary:
- speech and language activities as set up by the therapist
- daily speaking and listening
- mathematics extension, e.g. 'Springboard' or support
- additional literacy support (ALS)
- circle of friends activities
- circle time
- extra time using ICT with support
- counselling group
- individual in-class support for target achievement
- 'Reading Recovery'
- home–school book-bags/diaries
- nurture group placement
- phonological awareness programme
- paired reading
- social skills groups
- behaviour management

Secondary:
- circle of friends activities
- extra time using ICT with support
- group/individual counselling
- individual/group support for achieving targets
- paired reading
- touch typing
- 'buddy' system organisation
- study skills
- anger management group
- behaviour management programme
- support option – Key Stage 4

Activity 4: Provision mapping exercise

Primary

Year Group	Provision/resource for groups/individuals	Person(s)	Cost (SENCO will need help from SMT for this)
Nursery	✧		
Reception	✧		
Years 1/2	✧		
Years 3/4	✧		
Years 5/6	✧		

Activity 4: Provision mapping exercise

_S e c o n d a r y_			
Group	**Provision/resource for groups/individuals**	**Person(s)**	**Cost** (SENCO will need help from SMT for this)
Year 7	✧		
Year 8	✧		
Year 9	✧		
Year 10	✧		
Year 11	✧		

Activity 5: Support Policy Review

Reviewing your policy for managing support. You are asked to mark the following statements on a scale of 1–5.

Line a) According to your **ideal** view: 1 = *not necessary*; 5 = *highly necessary*
Line b) According to how you view **actual** practice at the moment: 1 = *not happening at all*;
          5 = *happening well*

Using the statements given below, mark your a) ideal, and b) actual practice ratings.

1. Learning Support Assistants (LSAs) have clearly written job descriptions provided when they start their job in the school.
    a) 1   2   3   4   5
    b) 1   2   3   4   5

2. LSAs have some form of induction training when they start their job in the school.
    a) 1   2   3   4   5
    b) 1   2   3   4   5

3. LSAs are managed by the SENCO or another named teacher.
    a) 1   2   3   4   5
    b) 1   2   3   4   5

4. LSAs have regular meetings with their class/subject teachers to plan lessons.
    a) 1   2   3   4   5
    b) 1   2   3   4   5

5. LSAs have some time for relevant preparation tasks.
    a) 1   2   3   4   5
    b) 1   2   3   4   5

6. LSAs appreciate the need for pupils to develop independence and to preserve their autonomy.
    a) 1   2   3   4   5
    b) 1   2   3   4   5

7. LSAs foster peer group acceptance.
    a) 1   2   3   4   5
    b) 1   2   3   4   5

8. LSAs have a clear understanding of their role as part of a team supporting teachers to support the pupils.
    a) 1   2   3   4   5
    b) 1   2   3   4   5

9. LSAs understand the use of supportive language when working with pupils.
    a) 1   2   3   4   5
    b) 1   2   3   4   5

10. LSAs know procedures for when class teacher is absent.
    a) 1   2   3   4   5
    b) 1   2   3   4   5

11. LSAs understand child protection issues and procedures.
    a) 1   2   3   4   5
    b) 1   2   3   4   5

12. LSAs are respected by teaching staff.
    a) 1   2   3   4   5
    b) 1   2   3   4   5

Now write your own additional sentence(s) to cover aspects of the policy and practice not listed above. Rate these in the same way on an a) and b) line.

Activity 6: Monitoring and Evaluation

This activity contains statements taken from either Circular 6/94 or the TTA National Standards Document about aspects of SEN coordination. These need to be photocopied and cut into strips. Each strip is to be given out to a pair of participants or a small group.

For each pair/group of participants, here are some points to think about (for your own school):

a) What underlying value system might be in operation?
b) What constraints might occur in implementation?
c) Write a target for this aspect of policy and practice.
d) Decide on success criteria.
e) Who will be responsible?
f) Decide on a reasonable time-scale.
g) How will it be monitored?

Choose targets for policy and practice which are feasible and can be monitored, i.e. 'Did it happen?', and evaluated, i.e. 'How effective was it?'

Pupil progress
Pupil progress is monitored by setting appropriate objectives and targets, and evaluating the effectiveness of teaching and learning.

or:
Pupil progress
Effective systems for monitoring and recording progress made by pupils with SEN are in place.

Pupil perspectives
Many schools have developed policies and procedures that encourage pupil involvement. (Code of Practice 2001, 2.4)

Discuss how far your school has achieved the aim of listening and taking account of pupil perspectives.

In-service training
Staff understand that the learning needs of pupils with SEN are supported through in-service training.

or:
In-service training
Staff have been given in-service training on the writing of IEPs which also helps their planning.

© Elizabeth Cowne, 2003

Resources

The policy describes the principles used by the school to allocate resources to and amongst pupils with SEN. The policy document explains how the governing body will ensure that funds help them to fulfil their duties under the 1993 Act.

Circular 6/94, Schedule 1.7

Discuss how far systems are in place for recording and monitoring the effective use of support.

Disability Discrimination

Schools will need to review their policies, practices and procedures to ensure they do not discriminate against disabled children. This means schools should not wait until a disabled child seeks admission in order to consider what reasonable adjustments they might make generally to meet the needs of disabled pupils.

DRC Code of Practice 6:13

Complaints

The policy makes clear to parents and children with SEN how they can make a complaint about provision and how this complaint will subsequently be dealt with by the school. Such information should include the time in which the school aims to respond.

Circular 6/94, Schedule 1.12

Parents

The school's policy contains a clear statement of the arrangement for ensuring close working partnerships with parents of children with SEN. These include recording parent concerns and involving parent views in assessment and reviewing IEPs. Parents are fully informed about the school's SEN procedures.

Circular 6/94, Schedule 1.15

Transitions

The school's arrangements are clearly stated concerning the transition of pupils between schools or between school and further education or adult life.

Circular 6/94, Schedule 1.16, Par. 54

Monitoring Success

The school's SEN policy sets out how the school proposes to demonstrate the effective implementation of its policy. The school indicates specific targets against which success of particular aspects is measured. These are to be reported annually to parents.

Circular 6/94, Schedule 1.11

Source Lists

Source List 1
Assessment Materials

(Unless otherwise stated all material is published by NFER/NELSON. Tel: 0845 602 1937)

Early years

Cameron, S. and White, M. (1987) *Portage Early Education Programme*. 0–6 years.
Clay, M. (1979) *Concepts of Print Test*. Beginning readers. Heinemann.
Clerebugh, J., Hart, K., Rider, K. and Turner, K. (1991) *Early Years, Easy Screen*. 4–5 years.
Downing, J., Schaefer, B. and Ayrs, D. (1994) *Larr Test of Emergent Literacy*. 3–5 years.
Lindsay, G. and Desforges, M. (1998) *Baseline Assessment: Practice, Problems and Possibilities*. London, David Fulton Publishers.
Pearson, L. and Quinn, J. (1980) *Bury Infant Checklist*. A development checklist for five year olds.

Tests of general ability

Dunn, L., Dunn, L. M., Whelton, C. and Pintile, D. (1997) *British Picture Vocabulary Scale (ii)*. 2–18 years.
Raven, J. C. (1998) *Raven's Progressive Matrices and Vocabulary Scales* (3 levels available).

Screening programmes

Robertson, A., Henderson, A., Fisher, J. and Gibson, M. (1995) *Quest (ii) – Identifying Children with Reading and Writing Difficulties*. 7–8 years.

Reading tests: individual

Bookbinder, G. (2000) *Salford Sentence Reading Test*, revised, 6–10. 6 years. London, Hodder and Stoughton.
Miller-Guron, L. (1999) *Wordchains*. Word reading screening test.
Neale, M. (1997) *Neale Analysis of Reading Ability*, 2nd edn, revised, 5–13 years.
Vincent, D., De la Mare, M. and Arnold, H. (1990) *Individual Reading Analysis*. 5/6–10 years.

Group reading tests

Group Reading Test (ii) (2000). For 6–14 years.

Material for miscue analysis

Arnold, H. (1995) *Diagnostic Reading Record*. London: Hodder and Stoughton.

Further Reading

Individual Education Plans, differentiation and circle time

Curry, M. and Bromfield, C. (1994) *Circle Time: Personal and social education for primary schools.* Tamworth: NASEN.

Edwards, S. (1998) *Modern Foreign Languages for All – Success for pupils with special educational needs.* Tamworth: NASEN.

Goldthorpe, M. (1998) *Effective IEPs Through Circle Time.* Wisbech: LDA.

Grove, N. (1998) *Literature for All: Developing literature in the curriculum for pupils with special educational needs.* London: David Fulton Publishers.

Malone, G. and Smith, D. (1996) *Learning to Learn – Developing study skills with children who have special educational needs.* Tamworth: NASEN.

Tilstone, C. *et al.* (2000) *Pupils with Learning Difficulties in Mainstream Schools.* London: David Fulton Publishers.

Tod, J., Castle, F. and Blamires, M. (1998) *IEPs – Implementing Effective Practice.* London: David Fulton Publishers.

IEP software

Csars software. *CSARS.* www.csars.co.uk/

Learn How Publications. *IEP Writer 2.* www.iepwriter.co.uk/iep_writer.htm

The Modbury Group. *Enable Software.* www.enable-online.com/

SEMERC/Granada Learning. *IEP Manager.* www.granadalearning.com

Literacy and numeracy

Beard, R. (1993) *Teaching Literacy: Balancing perspectives.* Bury St Edmunds: Hodder and Stoughton.

Berger, A. and Gross, J. (1999) *Teaching the Literacy Hour in an Inclusive Classroom: Supporting pupils with learning difficulties in a mainstream environment.* London: David Fulton Publishers.

Berger, A., Denise, M. and Portman, J. (2000) *Implementing the National Numeracy Strategy for Pupils with Learning Difficulties: Access to the daily mathematics lesson.* London: David Fulton Publishers.

DfEE (1999) *The National Literacy Strategy: Resources for supporting pupils with SEN during the literacy hour.* London: DfEE.

El-Naggar, O. (1996) *Specific Learning Difficulties in Mathematics: A classroom approach.* Tamworth: NASEN.

Fox, G. and Halliwell, M. (2000) *Supporting Literacy and Numeracy: A guide for LSAs.* London: David Fulton Publishers.

Henderson, A. (1998) *Maths for the Dyslexic – A practical guide.* London: David Fulton Publishers.

Hinson, M. (ed.) (1999) *Surviving the Literacy Hour.* Stafford: NASEN.

Morfett, C., edited by Higgs, J. and Gray, G. (1999) *Mathematics Assessment Pack.* London: SENSS, London Borough of Croydon.

National Literacy and Number Strategies, The (2002) *Including All Children in the Literacy Hour and Daily Mathematics Lesson.* DfES 0465/2002.

Pollock, J. and Waller, E. (1997) *Day-to-day Dyslexia in the Classroom.* London: Routledge.

Reason, R. and Boote, R. (1994) *Helping Children with Reading and Spelling: A special needs manual.* London: Routledge.

Riddick, B. (1996) *Living with Dyslexia - The social and emotional consequences of specific learning difficulties.* London: Routledge.

Sassoon, R. (1990) *Handwriting: A new perspective.* Leopard Learning.

Tod, J. (1999) *IEPs – Dyslexia.* London: David Fulton Publishers.

Emotional and behavioural difficulties

Bayley, J. and Haddock, L. (1999) *Training Teachers in Behavioural Management.* London: SENJIT.

Cornwall, J. and Tod, J. (1998) *IEPs – Emotional and Behavioural Difficulties.* London: David Fulton Publishers.

Kingston Friends Workshop Group (1996) *Ways and Means Today*. Kingston: KFWG.

Long, R. (1999) *Making Sense of Behaviour*. 8 booklets. Tamworth: NASEN.

Rogers, B. (2000) *Classroom Behaviour – A Practical Guide to Effective Teaching, Behaviour Management and Colleague Support*. London: Books Education.

Watkins, O. and Wagner, R. (2000) *Improving School Behaviour*. London: Paul Chapman.

Information about disabilities and disability issues

Cumine, V., Leach, J. and Stevenson, G. (1998) *Aspergers Syndrome: A practical guide for teachers*. London: David Fulton Publishers.

Hardy, C., Ogden, J., Newman, J. and Cooper, S. (2002) *Autism and ICT – A guide for teachers and parents*. London: David Fulton Publishers.

Martin, D. and Miller, C. (1999) *Language and the Curriculum*. London: David Fulton Publishers.

Pickles, P. (1998) *Managing the Curriculum for Children with Severe Motor Difficulties*. London: David Fulton Publishers.

Portwood, M. (1999) *Developmental Dyspraxia: Identification and intervention*, 2nd edn. London: David Fulton Publishers.

Saunders, S. (1999) *Fragile X Syndrome: A guide for teachers*. London: David Fulton Publishers.

Seach, D. (1998) *Autistic Spectrum Disorder: Positive approaches for teaching children with ASD*. Tamworth: NASEN.

Series: *Spotlight on Special Educational Needs*. Stafford: NASEN

    Beveridge, S. (1996) *Learning Difficulties*

    Dairies, B., Fleming, P. and Miller, C. (1996) *Speech and Language Difficulties*

    Fogell, J. and Long, R. (1997) *Emotional and Behavioural Difficulties*

    Kenward, H. (1996) *Physical Disabilities*

    Mason, H. (1996) *Visual Impairment*

    Smith, D. (1996) *Specific Learning Difficulties*

    Watson, L. (1996) *Hearing Impairment*

Thinking skills

Wallace, B. (ed.) (2001) *Teaching Thinking Skills Across the Primary Curriculum: A practical approach for all abilities*. London: David Fulton Publishers.

Policy-making

Audit Commission/ESTYN/Ofsted (2001) *Managing Special Educational Needs: A Self-review Handbook for Local Educational Authorities*. Audit Commission. www.audit-commission.gov.uk

Council for Disabled Children (1995) *Schools' SEN Policy Pack*. London: National Children's Bureau.

Gross, J. and White, A. (2003) *Special Educational Needs and School Improvement – Practical Strategies for Raising Standards*. London: David Fulton Publishers.

Ramjhun, A. F. (2002) *Implementing the Code of Practice for Children with Special Educational Needs: A practical guide*, 2nd edn. London: David Fulton Publishers.

Further education

Grove, B. and Saunders, G. (2003) 'Connecting with Connexions: the role of the personal adviser with young people with special educational and support needs', *Support for Learning*, February.

Maudslay, L. (2003) 'Policy changes in post-school learning for people with disabilities and learning difficulties and the implications for practice', *Support for Learning*, Vol.18, No.1, pp. 6–11.

Special needs assistants/training materials

Accredited training for support assistants is being organised in many LEAs. Courses are accredited by:
City and Guilds
The Open University
Various colleges using NVQ competencies courses. For further information ask your local further education college or your SEN Inspector.
Other sources of information include local libraries, careers centres, local Training and Enterprise councils.

Journals

Special Children

Questions Publishing Company, 27 Frederick Street, Hockley, Birmingham B13HH.

Support for Learning

NASEN Publications, NASEN House, 4/5 Amber Business Village, Amber Close, Arlington, Staffs B77 4RP. Tel: 01827 311500. Fax: 01827 313005.

British Journal of Special Education

NASEN Publications (as above).

SENCO Forum

(Mailbase website) www.mailbase.ak.uk
Or contact: Lydia Matheson, National Council for Educational Technology, Milburn Hill Road, Science Park, Coventry, CV4 7JJ.

SENCO Update

Optimus Publishing, 67–71 Goswell Road, London, EC1B 1LT.

Source List 2
Address List

Advisory Centre for Education (ACE) Ltd

Unit 1c, Aberdeen Studios, 22 Highbury Grove, London N5 2DQ
Admin. Tel: 020 7354 8318. Fax: 020 7354 9069
Exclusion line: 020 7704 9822
Adviceline: 0808 800 5793 (2–5 p.m. M–F)
website: www.ace-ed.org.uk
email: ace-ed@easynet.org.uk

ACE Centre Advisory Trust

92 Windmill Road, Headington, Oxford OX3 7DR
Tel: 01865 759800
Fax: 01865 759810
website: www.rmplc.co.uk/eduweb/sites/accent/index
email: info@ace-centre.org.uk (general enquiries)
[Equipment for disabled pupils]

Contact-a-Family

209–211 City Road, London EC1V 1JN
Tel: 020 7608 8700 and 0808 808 3555
Minicom: 020 7608 8702
website: www.cafamily.org.uk
email: info@cafamily.org.uk

Council for Disabled Children

c/o National Children's Bureau, 8 Wakley Street, London EC1V 7QE
Tel: 020 7843 6000
Fax: 020 7278 9512
email: membership@ncb.org.uk
website: www.ncb.org.uk

CSIE – Centre for Studies on Inclusive Education

Room ZS203, S Block, Frenchay Campus, Coldharbour Lane, Bristol BS16 1QU
Tel: 0117 344 4007
website: www.csie.org.uk

Disability Alliance

1st Floor East, Universal House, 88–94 Wentworth Street, London E1 7SA
Tel: 020 7247 8776
website: www.disabilityalliance.org/index.shtml.
[Publishers of the *Disability Rights Handbook*]

Disability Rights Commission

Tel: 08457 622633
website: www.drc-gb.org

Disabled Living Foundation

380–384 Harrow Road, London W9 2HU
Helpline: 0845 130 9177 (10–4pm M–F)
Tel: 020 7289 6111
website: www.dls.org.uk

Independent Panel for Special Education Advice (IPSEA)

6 Carlow Mews, Woodbridge, Suffolk IP12 1EA
Adviceline: 0800 0184016
General enquiries: 01394 380518
website: www.ipsea.org.uk

Invalid Children's Aid Nationwide (ICAN)

4 Dyer's Buildings, Holborn, London EC1N 2QP
Tel: 0870 010 4066
Fax: 0870 010 4067
website: www.ican.org.uk

National Association of Special Educational Needs (NASEN)

Membership Department and Publications, NASEN House, 4/5 Amber Business Village,
    Amber Close, Amington, Tamworth, Staffs, B77 4RP
Tel: 01827 311500
Fax: 01827 313005
website: www.nasen.org.uk

National Association of Toy and Leisure Libraries

68 Churchway, London NW1 1LT
Tel: 020 7387 9592
Fax: 020 7383 2714
website: www.natll.org.uk

National Portage Association

PO Box 3075, Yeovil, Somerset BA21 3FB
Tel: 01935 471641
website: www.portage.org.uk (includes list of regional contacts)
[Association works with parents of young disabled children]

Network 81

1–7 Woodfield Terrace, Chapel Hill, Stansted, Essex CM24 8AJ
Tel: 0870 770 3306
Admin: 0870 770 3262
website: www.network81.co.uk
[Parent support organisation – helpline, befrienders]

Parents for Inclusion

Unit 2, Ground Floor, 70 South Lambeth Rd, London SW8 1RL
Helpline: 020 7582 5008 (Tues, Wed, Thurs 10–12am and 1–3pm)
website: www.parentsforinclusion.org.uk
[Formerly Parents in Partnership]

Royal Association for Disability and Rehabilitation (RADAR)

12 City Forum, 250 City Road, London EC1V 8AF
Tel: 020 7250 3222
Fax: 020 7250 0212
website: www.radar.org.uk

Association for all Speech Impaired Children (AFASIC)

50–52 Great Sutton Street, London EC1V 0DJ
Tel: 020 7490 9410
Fax: 020 7251 2834
Helpline: 0845 355 5577 (M–F 11–2pm)
website: www.afasic.org.uk
email: info@afasic.org.uk

British Dyslexia Association

98 London Road, Reading, Berkshire RG1 5AU
Tel: 0118 966 8271
Fax: 0118 935 1927
Helpline: 0118 966 2677
website: www.bda-dyslexia.org.uk
email: info@dyslexiahelp-bda.demon.co.uk

Cystic Fibrosis Trust

11 London Road, Bromley, Kent BR1 1BY
Tel: 020 8464 7211
Fax: 020 8313 0472

Downs Syndrome Association (DSA)

155 Mitcham Road, London SW17 9PG
Tel: 020 8682 4001
Fax: 020 8682 4012
website: www.downs-syndrome.org.uk
email: downs-syndrome@org.uk

Epilepsy Action (British Epilepsy Association)

New Anstey House, Gate Way Drive, Yeadon, Leeds LS19 7XY
Tel: 0113 210 8800
Fax: 0113 391 0300
Helpline: 0808 800 5050 (Monday to Thursday 9–4.30pm, Friday 9–4pm)
website: www.epilepsy.org.uk
email: epilepsy@epilepsy.org.uk

MENCAP

115–123 Golden Lane, London EC1Y ORT
Tel: 020 7454 0454
Fax: 020 7608 3254
website: www.mencap.org.uk
email: mencap.plu@dial.pipex.com

MIND

Granta House, 15–19 Broadway, London E15 4BQ
Mind*info*line: 08457 660163 (M–F 9.15–5.15pm)
Fax: 020 8522 1725
website: www.mind.org.uk

National Autistic Society

393 City Road, London EC1V 1NG
Tel: 020 7833 2299
Fax: 020 7833 9666
website: www.nas.org.uk
email: nas@nasorg.uk

The National Institute of Conductive Education

Cannon Hill House, Russell Road, Birmingham B13 8RD
Tel: 0121 449 1569
Fax: 0121 449 1611
website: www.conductive-education.org.uk
email: foundation@conductive-education.org.uk

Royal National Institute for the Blind (RNIB)

105 Judd Street, London WC1H 9NE
Tel: 020 7388 1266
Tel: 0845 766 9999 (M–F 9–5pm)
Fax: 020 7388 2034
website: www.rnib.org.uk
email: webmaster@rnib.org.uk

Royal National Institute for the Deaf (RNID)

19–23 Featherstone Street, London EC1Y 8SL
Tel: 020 7296 8000. Textphone (London): 020 7296 8001
Freephone: 0808 808 0123. Textphone: 0808 808 9000
website: www.rnid.org.uk
email: informationline@rnid.org.uk

SCOPE (formerly the Spastics Society)

6 Market Rd, London N7 9PW
Tel: 020 7619 7100
Cerebral palsy helpline: 0808 800 3333 (M–F 9–9pm, 2–6pm weekends & BHs)
website: www.scope.org.uk
email: cphelpline@scope.org.uk

SENSE (UK deaf/blind charity)

11–13 Clifton Terrace, Finsbury Park, London N4 3SR
Tel: 020 7272 7774. Minicom: 020 7272 9848
Textphone: 020 7272 9648
Fax: 020 7272 6012
website: www.sense.org.uk
email: enquiries@sense.org.uk

SKILL (formerly the National Bureau for Students with Disabilities)

Head Office: Chapter House, 18–20 Crucifix Lane, London SE1 3JW
Infoline: 0800 328 5050 (voice)
           0800 068 2422 (text)
Minicom: 020 7450 0620
Fax: 020 7450 0650
website: www.skill.org.uk
email: skill@skill.org.uk

Appendices

These were listed as:

(a) blind pupils – pupils whose sight is so defective they require education by methods not using sight.
(b) partially sighted pupils – educated by special methods involving use of sight.
(c) deaf pupils.
(d) partially hearing pupils.
(e) educationally subnormal pupils.
(f) epileptic pupils – pupils who by reason of epilepsy cannot be educated under a normal regime.
(g) maladjusted pupils – emotional instability or disturbance.
(h) physically handicapped pupils.
(i) pupils suffering from speech defect.
(j) delicate pupils – pupils not falling under any other category who need a change of environment and who cannot without risk to health or educational development be educated under a normal regime of an ordinary school. (Handicapped Pupils and Special Schools Regulation 1959)

The largest category of children requiring special education was those described as educationally subnormal (ESN). These were children who were backward in basic subjects as well as those who were seen as 'dull'. Pupils with severe learning difficulties were not educated in schools at this time.

The Code of Practice (2001) divides those with SEN into 4 groups:
1. Cognition and Learning
   A – General Learning Difficulties
   B – Specific Learning Difficulties
2. Behavioural, Emotional and Social Difficulties
3. Communication and Interactive Difficulties
   A – Speech and Language Difficulties
   B – Autistic Spectrum Disorders
4. Sensory and Physical Difficulties
   A – Hearing Impairment
   B – Visual Impairment
   C – Physical and Medical Difficulties

**Appendix 2a
Governors'
Responsibilities**

The governing body must:

- do their best to secure that the necessary provision is made for any pupil who has SEN.

- ensure that, where the 'responsible person' – the head teacher or the appropriate governor – has been informed by the LEA that a pupil has SEN, those needs are known to all who are likely to teach him or her.

- ensure that teachers in the school are aware of the importance of identifying, and providing for, those pupils who have SEN.

- consult the LEA; as appropriate, the Funding Authority; and the governing bodies of other schools, when it seems to them necessary or desirable in the interests of coordinated special educational provision in the area as a whole.

- report annually to parents on the school's policy for pupils with SEN.

- ensure that the pupil joins in the activities of the school together with pupils who do not have SEN, so far as that is reasonably practical and compatible with the pupil receiving the necessary special educational provision, the efficient education of other children in the school and the efficient use of resources.

- have regard to the Code of Practice when carrying out their duties towards pupils with SEN.

(Education Act 1996 Sections 313, 317A)

Basic information about the school's special educational provision

1. The objectives of the governing body in making provision for pupils with special educational needs, and a description of how the governing body's special educational needs policy will contribute towards meeting those objectives.

2. The name of the person who is responsible for coordinating the day-to-day provision of education for pupils with special educational needs at the school (whether or not the person is known as the SENCO).

3. The arrangements which have been made for coordinating the provision of education for pupils with special educational needs at the school.

4. The admission arrangements for pupils with special educational needs who do not have a statement in so far as they differ from the arrangements for other pupils.

5. The kinds of provision for special educational needs in which the school specialises and any special units.

6. Facilities for pupils with special educational needs at the school including facilities which increase or assist access to the school by pupils who are disabled.

Information about the school's policies for the identification and assessment of, and provision for, all pupils with special educational needs

7. How resources are allocated to and among pupils with special educational needs.

8. How pupils with special educational needs are identified and their needs determined and reviewed.

9. Arrangements for providing access by pupils with special educational needs to a balanced and broadly based curriculum (including the National Curriculum).

10. How pupils with special educational needs engage in the activities of the school together with pupils who do not have special educational needs.

11. How the governing body evaluates the success of the education which is provided at the school to pupils with special educational needs.

12. Any arrangements made by the governing body relating to the treatment of complaints from parents of pupils with special educational needs concerning the provision made at the school.

Information about the school's staffing policies and partnership with bodies beyond the school

13. Any arrangements made by the governing body relating to in-service training for staff in relation to special educational needs.

14. The use made of teachers and facilities from outside the school, including links with support services for special educational needs.

15. The role played by the parents of pupils with special educational needs.

16. Any links with other schools, including special schools, and the provision made for the transition of pupils with special educational needs between schools or between the school and the next stage of life or education.

17. Links with child health services, social services and educational welfare services, and any voluntary organisations which work on behalf of children with special educational needs.

The Education (Special Educational Needs – Information) (England) Regulations 1999. Code of Practice (2001).

Appendix 3a
Guidance Notes on
Code of Practice
Forms and IEP Forms

Record of Concern

This form has proved popular with teachers for collating information about the pupil at early stages of concern. Information gathered should include:

● Health records
● Parents' views
● Previous school records
● Professional assessments and letters
● Observations
● Child's viewpoint.

The needs of the pupil at this stage will be met by differentiation of normal classroom work. This will be guided by information summarised on the Record of Concern. Action taken, other information to be sought and special arrangements made can be noted.

The Individual Education Plan form

Once information is collated from the Record of Concern and reviewed it may be clear that some pupils need a more detailed Individual Education Plan. Targets will be set which produce a working document which will inform the class teacher's planning. These will be:

● cross-curricular and related to the areas of concern;
● expressed in precise terms which can be assessed and evaluated;
● agreed with the pupil.

Step 1 – Collect information about the child from all previous records, interviews with parents, health checks, etc. Decide on the major areas of concern and record these. Write down the child's strengths and present known levels of attainment. Discuss the learning difficulties or problem areas with the pupil as well as finding out what they feel they can do well. Note any special pastoral and medical arrangements.

Step 2 – Decide on targets for the present plan; these should be as cross-curricular as necessary but as precise as possible. They should be expressed as clear observable behaviours, if not it will be difficult to measure success in reaching the target. Avoid 'fuzzies' like 'Sean needs to learn to write.' Express this as 'Sean will write three sentences unaided with no more than 3 errors.'

Step 3 – Decide teaching strategies to achieve the targets; include frequency and type of support to be given and any specialist resources needed, or particular contexts required.

Step 4 – Decide on success criteria for each target and how it will be assessed. Link to National Curriculum assessment where possible.

Step 5 – Important – Set review date and when it comes round, review the success or otherwise in reaching the targets. Parents' and pupils' views should be recorded.

Step 6 – Set new targets or repeat those already used. Modify support levels, change teaching strategies or success criteria as necessary. It will be better to set achievable targets.

Step 7 – Teach to new targets.

An IEP is a process over time. Show as much precise information as possible about what the child can do and what support level is needed to achieve success. Parents should be asked to the review and their views recorded on the form or in other ways as the school policy dictates.

Record of Concern at Stage 1

Child's name   Class teacher   Date of Report

_____   _____   _____

Sheet number:

_____   _____

DoB:	Age:	NC Year:	Class:

Concerns (Check health records; ask parents' views)

Present levels of attainment/development – pupil's strengths

Action

Review date

Outcome of review

Individual Education Plan

Date of plan   Child's name   Plan number

_____   _____   _____

Teacher's name   Date of IEP Review or Annual Review (Stage 5)

_____   _____

Pupil's views	Parents' views

Pupil's strengths and attainments	Areas of concern

Learning targets _state these precisely_	Teaching strategies; frequency of support	How progress will be assessed and monitored

Review outcomes

Appendix 3b
The Relationship
between Bilingual
Learners' Language
Stages and Code of
Practice Stages

Bilingual learners are often classified by EAL teachers by their stages of development in learning English. This should not be confused with the Code of Practice graduated response.

Bilingual stages

Stage 1 – new to English
Stage 2 – learning familiarity with English
Stage 3 – becoming confident in use of English
Stage 4 – on the way to fluent use of English in most social learning contexts.

Things to do

- Find out how long the pupil has been learning English.
- Talk to parents about the child in the home context and what language(s) are spoken at home.
- Check health records and previous educational history.

Read *Assessing the Needs of Bilingual Pupils* by Deryn Hall, published by David Fulton Publishers, 2001.

Pupils at bilingual Stage 1 should not be given an IEP unless they have clearly identified disabilities. Pupils at bilingual Stage 1 will often be supported by teachers from a bilingual service (EMAG). It takes up to two years to develop basic interpersonal communication. EMAG teachers can give advice on how to support and teach these pupils to acquire their new language while retaining the use of their own first language.

*Appendix 4a
Instrumental
Enrichment: Cognitive
Functions as
Expressed by Students*

1. INPUT – Gathering all the information we need
- using senses to gather, clear and complete information
- using a plan so we don't miss anything
- giving all of this a name so we can talk about it
- describing things in terms of where and when they occur
- deciding on characteristics which stay the same
- organising the information we gather by considering more than one thing at a time
- being precise and accurate when it matters.

2. ELABORATION – Using the information we have gathered
- defining a problem, what we must do and what we must figure out
- using only that part of the information that is relevant
- having a picture in our mind of what we are looking for and what we aim to do
- making a plan which will involve steps needed to reach our goal
- remembering various pieces of information we will need
- looking for relationships
- comparing objects or experiences
- finding categories or sets
- thinking about 'what if' questions
- using logic to defend our opinions.

3. OUTPUT – Expressing the solution to a problem
- being clear and precise so you can be understood
- thinking things through before you answer and waiting before you say something you may regret
- not panicking if you cannot immediately answer a question, return to it later
- carrying a picture in your mind for comparison without losing or changing details.

(Adapted from Adey and Shayer 1994)

Feuerstein *et al.* (1980) lists the nature and focus of cognitive impairments related to his three phases of information processing: Input, Elaboration and Output. These include lack of planning, impulsive behaviour, impaired receptive verbal tools, impaired spatial orientation or temporal concepts, inability to define a problem or pursue logical evidence. It is his programme of instrumental enrichment which is designed to overcome these impaired processes and blocked learning.

Appendix 4b
Summary of Bloom's
Taxonomy

Level 1: Acquiring knowledge

The learner is given information, specific terminology or symbols; the learner masters specific techniques or skills. Acquiring knowledge involves memory, repetition and description. Knowing where and how to find out information is one of the important requisites of knowledge acquisition. Very able pupils need far less time to absorb knowledge and less rehearsal to reach mastery level in skills. Pupils with learning difficulties will need more guidance in making connections, more rehearsal and practice.

Level 2: Comprehension

The learner is required to demonstrate that knowledge has been acquired by:
- *Translation* – explaining meanings and selecting information to answer questions.
- *Interpretation* – interpreting and reordering facts, contrasting or classifying these according to specific criteria.
- *Extrapolation* – determining consequences and implications.

The first of these ways, *translation*, is the most commonly used by teachers. Predicting outcomes and discussing implications may require working at a higher level of thinking.

Level 3: Application

The learner is required to:

- Use knowledge to solve problems
- Translate methods and techniques to new solutions.

Bring general principles to bear in new questions.

Level 4: Analysis

The learner is involved in breaking down the whole to clarify the relationships between constituent parts. This involves:

- Differentiating fact from fiction
- Identifying hidden meanings
- Finding themes and patterns
- Understanding systems and organisations.

Level 5: Synthesis

The learner is required to create new relationships, combine elements to form a new whole. This involves:

- Organising sets of ideas to make new statements
- Developing plans to test a hypothesis
- Creating a new form of classifying data
- Discovering new relationships
- Inventing, changing and improving ideas
- Thinking creatively and risk making new connections.

Level 6: Evaluation

The learner goes through a process of appraising, assessing and criticising which involves:

- Judging on the basis of logical evidence
- Verifying the worth of evidence or proof
- Evaluation according to specified criteria
- Comparing contrasting theories or generalisations
- Arbitrating in controversial arguments.

This requires personal decision-making based on reasoned and logical argument, supported by evidence.
(Adapted from Bloom 1965)

Appendix 9a
Statement of Special
Educational Needs:
Appendices

A: parental advice

B: educational advice (usually from the school but specialist teachers' advice may be added where applicable)

C: medical advice (doctors and therapists)

D: psychological advice

E: advice from the Social Services Authority (this is not completed if the child is not known to Social Services)

F: other advice obtained by the authority

G: advice obtained by the authority since the last assessment of the child under section 323 of the Education Act 1996 was made.

(See Code of Practice (2001) Schedule 2. Regulation 16, p. 43)

Statements that were written before the Code of Practice (2001) will have different letters, as used in the Code of Practice (1994).

Appendix 9b
The SEN
Management Form

This is for the SENCO to use when collating information onto one form for easy reference. Once opened it can be updated as necessary. Only one form is needed per pupil, this cuts down unnecessary copying of information onto the frequently changing classroom IEP form. The form should record:

- National Curriculum year
- Schools attended
- Outside services and agencies involved with dates of reports or advice given
- IEP review dates

Only for a few pupils:
- Dates for a statutory assessment request
- Date of statutory assessment starting
- Date of draft statement
- Dates of annual reviews.

Information which will not change over time could also be recorded on this form: for example, the mother tongue spoken by the child, how long English has been spoken and the position in the family. This will vary according to school policy.

SEN Management Form

Child's name _____ Date of birth _____ NC Year _____

Names of those with
parental responsibility _____

Schools attended	LEA

Outside agency and support service involvement

Agency / Support service involvement	Date of report

Dates	IEP Reviews Notes	Other dates and annual reviews

*Appendix 10a
Different Ways of
Observing Children*

Observation is a way of finding out more, but first it is necessary to ask *Why observe?* Answers could be:

● As a means of generating hypotheses.
● As a means of answering specific questions. How often does a child do that?
● As a way to better understand children and their viewpoints and behaviours.

This last point is the most relevant to those wishing to learn about pupil perspectives.

Next ask *What should we observe?*

This could be a matter of choosing the scale of the focus, either:

● Large units of activity, e.g. playground behaviour, or
● Specific activities, e.g. reading strategies, or
● Facial expressions, gestures, eye movements within specific contexts.

Next ask *How should the observations be done?*

They could be in the form of:

● Diaries; biographies over time, e.g. day, week.
● Single episode recording.
● Time sampling, e.g. one minute every 15 minutes.
● Event sampling; record specific type of event wherever it happens.
● Tracking; observing child in different contexts or with different adults over a fixed period.

What form will recording take?

● Narrative descriptions.
● Prepared checklists to tick or mark with symbols.
● Audio or video tape analysis.

All have advantages and some suit certain techniques best. Narrative is necessary for diaries, tracking and events sampling. Checklists are best for time sampling. A mixture of methods may produce the best all-round picture.

Cautions:
● All observations take time – analysis can be even more time consuming.
● Focus as much as possible; be selective but be aware of bias from this selection.
● Note what you see, not your inferences; draw no conclusions without evidence.
● Be aware of observer bias – two observers may produce a clearer picture of reality.
● Try to see things from the pupil's perspective, not yours.
● Prepare carefully to avoid missing things because you cannot record quickly or accurately enough.
● Warn colleagues of your activities and do not underestimate pupils. They might ask 'What are you doing?' if your behaviour is too peculiar!
● What part will spoken language play? Will this be recorded with the observation and if so, how?
● How valid are your observations? Can you check these with the child?

Examples

Time sampling

● Useful when behaviours to be observed are frequent.
● Or when behaviours are distinct and recognised early.

Advantages

- It takes less time if prepared well.
- Provides quantifiable data.
- Useful for baseline information.

Disadvantages

- Doesn't tell much about pupil perspectives.
- Omits context and interaction between behaviours.
- Can distort reality because cause and effect may not be noted.

Event sampling

- Useful to learn more about a selective type of behaviour in detail.
- Or when a whole event can be recorded and analysed.
- Where context can be noted, such as antecedents and consequences can be noted – good for the ABC analysis of behaviour.
- Can be used for infrequent events.
- Pupil views can be included.

Disadvantages

- More difficult to prepare for thoroughly.
- Needs more analysis after the observation.

Tracking

- Useful for finding out the effect of different teachers and different experiences on a child to discover reasons for a problem.

Disadvantages

- Taking the time to do this may be difficult.
- Colleagues need to agree and understand purposes.
- Being inconspicuous may be difficult. The observer may make pupil behaviours different.
- Focus on one pupil might be difficult to disguise and could cause embarrassment. Observer's activity must be plausible to the peer group.

The best way may be to use a mixture of techniques and data and to balance one with another. *Remember* observation material is confidential and must be used to provide information to solve a problem or gain useful information *to help the child or children*. Once used it should not be kept in any way that could identify the pupil. Pupils and parents have rights. Ask permission of parents, if at all possible. Observation will provide data, set up hypotheses and is one source of information, but pupils' views will need to be collected as well as the views of parents and other professionals to check out its validity.

Appendix 10b
Example of
Questionnaire for
Primary Pupils

Use the faces to find out how children feel about your area of enquiry. Ask your questions orally and use the first two to get the group used to the idea of colouring in or ticking the face that is most like 'how they feel when...', for example, watching their favourite TV programme. Then ask about 'how they feel when...' using the research questions. (Used by the ILEA Research for eight year olds looking into pupils' views about learning to read and write from ILEA Research and Statistics 1988.)

Appendix 10c
Definition of a Parent
from Glossary of Code
and the Children Act
1989

A parent includes any person:

- Who is not a natural parent of the child but who has parental responsibility for him or her, or
- Who has care of the child.

Parental responsibility under Section 2 of the Children Act falls upon:

- All mothers and fathers who were married to each other at the time of the child's birth.
- Mothers who were not married to the father at the time of the child's birth.
- Fathers who were not married to the mother at the time of the child's birth, but who have parental responsibility either by agreement with the child's mother or through a court order.

References

Adey, P. and Shayer, M. (1994) *Really Raising Standards: Cognitive intervention and academic achievement.* London: Routledge.

Ainscow, M. and Tweddle, D. (1988) *Encouraging Classroom Success.* London: David Fulton Publishers.

Audit Commission/HMI (1992) *Getting the Act Together – Provision for pupils with special educational needs: A management handbook for schools and local education authorities.* London: HMSO.

Balshaw, M. H. (1999) *Help in the Classroom,* 2nd edn. London: David Fulton Publishers.

Blagg, N., Ballinger, M. and Gardner, R. (1988) *Somerset Thinking Skills.* Oxford: Blackwell/Somerset County Council.

Bloom, B. A. (1965) *Taxonomy of Educational Objectives.* London: Longman.

Booth, T., Ainscow, M., Black-Hawkins, K., Vaughan, M. and Shaw, L. (2000) *Index for Inclusion: Developing learning and participation in schools.* London: The Centre for Studies in Inclusive Education.

Briggs, M. (2000) 'Feel free to be flexible', *Special Children* **125**.

Bruner, J. (1968) *Towards a Theory of Instruction.* New York: W. W. Norton.

Buck, D. and Davis, V. (2001) *Assessing Pupils' Performance using the P Scales.* London: David Fulton Publishers.

Campbell, K. (1995) 'How schools might work more effectively with social service departments', Discussion Paper V, 7–11, *Schools' SEN Policy Pack.* London: National Children's Bureau.

Cowne, E. A. (1993) 'Conversational uses of the Repertory Grid for personal learning and the Management of Change in Special Educational Needs.' Unpublished PhD thesis. Uxbridge: Brunel University.

Cowne, E. A. and Murphy, M. (2000) *A Beginner's Guide to SEN: A handbook.* Tamworth: NASEN.

Cowne, E. A. (2003) *Developing Inclusive Practice: The SENCO's Role in Managing Change.* London: David Fulton Publishers.

Dale, N. (1996) *Working with Families with Special Needs: Partnership and practice.* London: Routledge.

Dearing, R. (1994) *The National Curriculum and its Assessment.* London: SCAA.

DES (1944) *Education Act.* London: HMSO.

DES (1959) *Handicapped Pupils and Special Educational Needs Regulations.* London: HMSO.

DES (1970) *Handicapped Children Act.* London: HMSO.

DES (1978) *Special Educational Needs: Report of the committee of enquiry into the education of handicapped children and young people.* (The Warnock report). London: HMSO.

DES (1980) *Education Act.* London: HMSO.

DES (1981) *Education Act.* London: HMSO.

DES (1983) *Assessment and Statements of Special Educational Needs,* Joint Circular with DHSS and LEAs. Circular 1/83. London: HMSO.

DES (1983, 1984, 1985) *The In-service Training Grants Scheme,* Circulars 3/83, 4/84, 5/85. London: HMSO.

DES (1986) *Education Act.* London: HMSO.

DES, Black, P. J. (1987) *Task Group on Assessment and Testing – A report.* London: HMSO.

DES (1988) *Education Reform Act.* London: HMSO.

DfE (1992) *The Education Act.* London: HMSO.

DfE (1993) *The Education Act.* London: HMSO.

DfE (1994a) *The Code of Practice on the Identification and Assessment of Special Educational Needs.* London: HMSO.

DfE (1994b) *Special Educational Needs: A guide for parents.* London: HMSO.

DfE (1994c) *The Organisation of Special Education.* Circular 6/94. London: HMSO.

DfEE (1996) *The Education Act.* London: HMSO.

DfEE (1997) *The SENCO Guide.* London: DfEE Publications.

DfEE (1998a) *The National Literacy Strategy: A framework for teaching.* London: DfEE Publications.

DfEE (1998b) *The National Numeracy Strategy: Framework for teaching mathematics for reception to Year 6.* London: DfEE Publications.

DfEE (1998c) *Programme for Action.* London: HMSO.

DfEE (1999) *Social Inclusion: Pupil Support.* Circular 10/99. London: DfEE Publications.

DfES (2001a) *Special Educational Needs Disability Act (SENDA).* London: The Stationery Office.

DfES (2001b) *Special Educational Needs Code of Practice –* No. 581. London: DfES Publications.

DfES (2001c) *SEN Toolkit –* No. 558. London: DfES Publications.

DfES (2001d) *Inclusive Schooling –* No. 0774. London: DfES Publications.

DfES (2002) *Accessible Schools: Planning to increase access to schools for disabled pupils.* LEA/0168. London: DfES Publications.

DHSS (1989) *The Children Act.* London: HMSO.

Diamond, D. C. (1995) 'How to get the best from your flexible friend – a review of the working relationship between schools and SEN support services', *Support for Learning* **10**(2), 63–9.

Disability Rights Commission (1995) *Disability Discrimination Act.* London: HMSO.

Donaldson, M. (1978) *Children's Minds.* Glasgow: Fontana.

DRC (2002a) *Code of Practice for Schools.* Disability Rights Commission. London: The Stationery Office.

DRC (2002b) *Code of Practice for Post 16.* Disability Rights Commission. London: The Stationery Office.

FEFC (1996) *Inclusive Learning, the Report of the Learning Difficulties and/or Disabilities Committee.* (The Tomlinson Report). Coventry: Further Education Funding Council.

Feuerstein, R., Rand, Y., Hoffman, M. and Miller, R. (1980) *Instrumental Enrichment – An intervention programme for cognitive modifiability.* Baltimore, MD: University Park Press.

Fish, J. (1989) *What is Special Education?* Milton Keynes: Open University Press.

Florian, L. (1998) 'Inclusive practice', in Tilstone, C., Florian, L. and Rose, R. *Promoting Inclusive Practice.* London: Routledge.

Fox, G. (1998) *A Handbook for Learning Support Assistants: Teachers and assistants working together.* London: David Fulton Publishers.

Galloway, D. (1985) *Schools, Pupils and Special Educational Needs.* London: Croom Helm.

Gascoigne, E. (1995) *Working with Parents as Partners in SEN.* London: David Fulton Publishers.

George, D. (1997) *The Challenge of the Able Child*, 2nd edition. London: David Fulton Publishers.

Gipps, C. (1992) *What We Know about Effective Primary Teaching.* London: Institute of Education and Tufnell Press.

Gross, J. and Berger, A. (2002) *A Reliable Guide.* Special Spring edition.

Hall, D. (2001) *Assessing the Needs of Bilingual Pupils,* 2nd edition. London: David Fulton Publishers.

Hanko, G. (1995) *Special Needs in Ordinary Classrooms: From staff support to staff development*, 3rd edition. London: David Fulton Publishers.

Hart, S. (1991) 'The collaborative classroom', in McLaughlin, C. and Rouse, M. *Supporting Schools.* London: David Fulton Publishers.

Hart, S. (1995) 'Down a different path', Discussion Paper I, 33–42, *Schools' SEN Policy Pack.* London: National Children's Bureau.

Inhelder, B. and Piaget, J. (1958) *The Growth of Logical Thinking.* London: Routledge and Kegan Paul.

Lipman, M., Sharp, M. and Oscanyan, F. (1980) *Philosophy in the Classroom.* Philadelphia: Temple University Press.

Lorenz, S. (1998) *Effective In-Class Support.* London: David Fulton Publishers.

Mallett, R. (1995) 'Parents: SEN policy and practice', Discussion Paper IV, 7–12, *Schools' SEN Policy Pack.* London: National Children's Bureau.

McKeown, S. (2000) 'Reading the signs', *Special Children,* **125**, 17–19.

McKeown, S. (2003) 'Helping hand', *TES, The Teacher,* 31 January, 16–17.

National Curriculum Council (1989) *Implementing the National Curriculum – Participation by pupils with SEN*, Circular No. 5. York: NCC.

Norwich, B. (1990a) *Reappraising Special Education.* London: Cassell.

Norwich, B. (1990b) 'How entitlement can become a restraint', in Daniels, H. and Ware, J. *Special Educational Needs and the National Curriculum.* London: Kogan Page and University of London, Institute of Education.

Norwich, B. (1995) 'Individual Education Plans', Discussion Paper II, 23–30, *Schools' SEN Policy Pack.* London: National Children's Bureau.

Ofsted (1996a) *Promoting High Achievement for Pupils with SEN.* London: HMSO.

Ofsted (1996b) *The SEN Code of Practice: 1 year on.* London: HMSO.

Ofsted (1997) *The SEN Code of Practice: 2 years on.* London: HMSO.

Ofsted (1999) *The SEN Code of Practice: 3 years on. The contribution of Individual Education Plans to the raising of standards for pupils with special educational needs.* London: HMSO.

O'Hanlon, C. (1993) 'Changing the school by reflectively re-defining the role of the special needs co-ordinator', in Dyson, A. and Gains, C. (eds) *Rethinking Special Needs in Mainstream Schools Towards the Year 2000*, 99–109. London: David Fulton Publishers.

QCA (1999) *The Revised National Curriculum.* London: QCA.

QCA/DfEE (2000) *Curriculum Guidance for the Foundation Stage.* London: QCA.

QCA (2001) *Supporting the Target Setting Process.* London: QCA.

Reason, R. and Boote, R. (1994) *Helping Children with Reading and Spelling: A Special Needs Manual.* London: Routledge.

Rieser, R. (1995) 'Developing a whole school approach to inclusion: making the most of the Code of Practice and the 1993 Act: A personal view', Discussion Paper III, 39–46. *Schools' SEN Policy Pack.* London: National Children's Bureau.

Robertson, C. (1999) 'Initial teacher education and inclusive schooling', *Support for Learning*, **14**(4), 169–73.

Russell, P. (1995) 'The transition plan', Discussion Paper IV, 57–65. *Schools' SEN Policy Pack*. London: National Children's Bureau.

School Curriculum and Assessment Authority (SCAA) (1996) *Supporting Pupils with SEN: Key Stage 3*. London: SCAA.

Skinner, B. F. (1974) *About Behaviourism*. London: Jonathan Cape.

Sproson, B. (2003) 'Solution or smoke screen – the use of further education colleges in making KS4 provision for difficult to manage (D2M) students', *Support for Learning*, **18**(1), 18–23.

Sutton, A. (1982) 'The powers that be', *Unit 8, E241 Course Material*. Milton Keynes: Open University Press.

Teacher Training Agency (TTA) (1998) *National Standards for Special Educational Needs Co-ordinators*. London: Teacher Training Agency.

Thomas, G. (1992) *Effective Classroom Teamwork*. London: Routledge.

Tizard, B. and Hughes, M. (1984) *Young Children Learning*. Glasgow: Fontana.

Tomlinson, S. (1982) *A Sociology of Special Education*. London: Routledge and Kegan Paul.

Vygotsky, L. S. (1978) *Mind in Society*. Massachusetts: Harvard University Press.

Wall, K. (2003) 'Pupils with Special Needs and the National Literacy Strategy – an analysis of the literature', *Support for Learning*, **18**(1), 35–41.

Wedell, K. (1980) 'Early identification and compensatory interaction', in Knights, R. M. and Bakker, D. J. *Treatment of Hyperactive and Learning Disordered Children*. Baltimore: University Park Press.

Weller, K. and Craft, A. (1983) *Making up Our Minds: An exploratory study of Instrumental Enrichment*. London: Schools Council Publications.

Wragg, E. C. (1997) *The Cubic Curriculum*. London: Routledge.

Index